# When
# Chicken
# Soup
# is Not Enough

# When
# Chicken
# Soup
## is Not Enough

Learn How to Create a
Healing Miracle in Your Life!

Revolutionary Healing Through
the Mind-Body Connection

## by RALPH E. RETHERFORD, M.D.

Frederick Fell Publishers, Inc.
2131 Hollywood Blvd., Suite 305, Hollywood, FL 33020
Phone: (954) 925-5242    Fax: (954) 925-5244
**Web Site: www.Fellpub.com**

# Frederick Fell Publishers, Inc.

2131 Hollywood Boulevard, Suite 305
Hollywood, Florida 33020
954-925-5242
**E-mail: Fellpub@aol.com**
**Visit our Web site at www.Fellpub.com**

Published by Frederick Fell Publishers, Inc., 2131 Hollywood, Blvd., Suite 305,
Hollywood, Florida 33020.

This publication is designed to provide accurate and authoritative information in regard to the
subject matter covered. *This book is not intended to replace the advice and guidance of a
trained physician nor is it intended to encourage self-treatment of illness or medical disease.
Although the case histories presented are true, all names of patients have been changed.*

**Library of Congress Cataloging-in Publication Data**
Retherford, Ralph E.
      When chicken soup is not enough  :  revolutionary healing through the mind-body
connection  /  by Ralph E. Retherford.
    p.  cm.
    Includes index.
    ISBN 0-88391-085-3
    1. Mind and body. 2. Psychophysiology.  I. Title.
    BF161 .R   1999, 2002
    616.08--dc21

10 9 8 7 6 5 4 3 2

99-23906
CIP

Art Director: Elena Solis

# Table of Contents

# III. YOU CAN UNLOCK THE DOOR TO PERMANENT WELLNESS!

℞

# Acknowledgements

Many people have helped me in the process of bringing this book into print. For urging me to write this book in the first place, I would like to thank Judy Tatelbaum. I'd also like to thank her for her generous help in the initial editing and finding an agent, but especially for her refusal to let me quit when difficult times forced me to put the project on the back burner.

For his enthusiasm about my ideas on mind-body interactions in the workplace, I extend my heartfelt thanks to my associate and mentor Hank Calero. His encouragement and hard work produced an innovative seminar series on this material and helped me format the section on work-related illness and injuries. Duane Newcomb provided invaluable help with his experienced editor's pen, fearlessly paring down the book to its present form. His belief in the value of my message came at a key time. I want to thank the Men's Group of Carmel for their wisdom and support throughout the writing of the manuscript.

Special thanks go to my dear friend Steve Harmer whose friendship has sustained me through hard times, and who introduced my work to Hugo Gerstl at Millennium Publishing. I want to thank Hugo for his wonderful enthusiasm for the book, and for finding a home for the manuscript with Frederick Fell Publishers, Inc. I owe thanks to my publisher, Don Lessne, for taking a chance, and to Callie Oettinger for her capable editing.

Finally, I want to thank the thousands of patients whose willingness to open up to me about their personal lives continues to teach me about the mind-body connection.

ℭℜ

# Introduction

*...And then he said that in another castle the daughter
was ill and they knew no remedy that would cure her.*

*Oh, the fools!* said the Griffin. *Under the cellar steps a toad has made
its nest of her hair and if she got her hair back, she would be well.*

**—The Griffin, Grimm's Fairy Tales**

I n the summer of 1970, when I graduated from the University of
California Medical School in San Francisco, the formal stage of
my medical education ended. For the previous four years I had
received the best instruction available on how the human body
works. I had dissected cadavers, peered through microscopes at
bacteria, and studied the core curriculum: anatomy, biochemistry,
microbiology, pathology, physiology, neuroanatomy, parasitology,
and histology, as well as a few other *ologies* I'm sure I've since
forgotten. This training turned me into a high-tech repairman qualified
to figure out what is going wrong with a patient's body when it
becomes sick. I became a fix-it-all — what we all want and expect
our doctor to be. We want him or her to peer knowledgeably into our
body's orifices, feel for swollen glands or lumps that should not be
there, order some tests or scans, and finally report back. We want
our doctor to prescribe medicine that will make things better, or
maybe even eliminate the problem altogether. After all, we don't
have time for this nonsense of being sick.

When you think about it, this sounds a lot like taking your car to
the garage for repairs. You describe the noise or vibration. The
mechanic hooks it to his diagnostic devices, zeros in on the problem,
and fixes it. It's that simple.

Surely you ought to be able to do the same thing with your body.
After all, it is just a sophisticated, biophysical machine that is designed
to carry you around, while you attend to your affairs. Or is it?

There is, like it or not, a fundamental difference between cars and people, a difference that my professors never talked about. Unlike people, cars don't have feelings; they are just mechanical devices that don't need to be convinced to stop using the wrong kind of oil. They don't quit running after an accident just because they're afraid to go back out on the freeway. They don't get jealous if you drive your friend's new Porsche. They don't feel like they've gotten a raw deal when you forget to put in premium gas. They don't get ulcers when they're caught for two hours in a traffic bottleneck and they don't get angry when a jerk leaves a dent in their fender.

This idea that your body is simply a mechanical gadget that can be fixed like a car causes a lot of trouble. Why? The answer is that, fundamentally it is not true. This part I learned in the second half of my medical education — the half that was self-taught. Most experienced medical doctors agree that a large percentage of their patients' medical problems are related to their emotions. This means what's been going on in your life — your job, your family life, your love life, or other personal affairs — can make your body sick.

So what's new? Everyone knows that stress causes illness, perhaps, but when we get sick, we almost always have trouble relating our illness to the stress in our lives. Why? Because our defenses tend to hide the truth from us.

Most of us never consider that stress causes our medical problems. We always want a physical cause, because we don't want to think that *it's all in our head* or that we are somehow responsible for our own illness.

Often we connect our illness, or our aches and pains, to various physical factors, like an infection or twisting the wrong way. A common one is: *Oh, I've caught the bug that's going around.* Another is: *I knew I shouldn't have gone outside while my hair was still wet.* Still another: *I knew I shouldn't have lifted that heavy box.*

Sometimes we are right. Many of our ailments are due to purely physical factors like physical injury, inherited problems, lack of exercise, food poisoning, too much rich food, vitamin or mineral imbalances, infections, or exposure to toxic substances. But, an equal or greater number of health problems are due to stress.

Most people believe that if they could just relax, slow down, and adopt a more positive attitude, all stress-related illnesses would disappear. This is an oversimplification of the way our minds and bodies work together, because most stress-related illnesses spring from stress that is submerged in our unconscious through the action of our defense mechanisms. We are genuinely unaware that anything is bothering us — this is the heart of the problem.

Often, when we get sick it is a sign that we have run into trouble. Rather than facing the situation squarely, we deal with it by ignoring it. Then it goes underground and creates havoc in our health. Getting well may involve learning to say *no* more often, or admitting when we are upset or angry, and doing something to resolve our feelings. Thus, illness is often an opportunity to learn and grow. If we don't figure out how to do that, we will stay stuck in the same pattern.

Western medicine looks to our physical bodies for answers, but many ailments remain mysterious and resistant to treatment, if not incurable. To balance this approach, we need to begin shifting our focus from physical causes to emotional ones, and understand that many of today's common ailments have their roots in mind-body interactions.

How do you do this? By learning how the mind-body connection works. The way your body responds to your innermost needs, feelings and beliefs follows simple, easy-to-understand principles that should have been taught in grammar school.

Before you begin, it's important to realize that all of us get disturbing symptoms that are the result of our bodies responding to events in our lives. That is the most normal thing in the world. You may get a dry mouth before giving a speech, or lose your appetite before a date.

While some of us have more of a tendency to develop stress-related physical symptoms than others, none of us are immune. When you do get symptoms, it's important to understand that it is not your fault. You have no control over your unconscious patterns and you don't intentionally bring those symptoms on yourself. Nor do you imagine them. They happen because of deeper forces within you.

If you are tired of going to various health practitioners for one quick fix after another, this book offers you a way to regain control over your own health. Once you learn how your symptoms connect to what's going on in your life, you can begin a process of self-exploration and self-healing. Since it is difficult to evaluate yourself clearly, I recommend that you do this with the help of a health practitioner who knows how to work with the mind-body connection.

Unlike other books that deal with stress and illness, this one clearly explains the critical role that your unconscious mind plays in creating illness and injury, and teaches you how to deal with it.

*—Ralph E. Retherford, M.D.*

# Section I

# What Makes Us Sick

# 1 How Emotions Convert into Physical Symptoms

lthough almost everybody seems to know that stress can cause illness, I've met very few people who can tell me what stress is. Is it feeling rushed? Is it losing sleep? Is it being scared? Angry? Upset? Or overworked? Maybe it's all of the above. Even fewer people have been able to tell me what kind of stress makes people sick and what kind of sickness stress causes.

Stress is supposed to cause headaches, yet many people with headaches deny there is any stress in their lives. Others go through tremendous stress, yet stay in perfect health. Because part of the reason for this fuzzy thinking about the stress-illness connection is the confusion surrounding the exact meaning of stress, I'm going to eliminate it in this chapter and talk about unhappiness instead.

Often, when something makes you unhappy, you are more vulnerable and may become sick or injured. The real rub comes when you are unhappy inside, and hide the unhappiness from yourself. Upon close examination, you'll see this unhappiness falls into a relatively small number of general categories. (We will examine these in detail later in this book.) Although most of us usually do okay if we are aware of our unhappiness, it is when we are unaware that problems occur. Let me give you an example:

## The Case of the Cat's Meow

Jerry wasn't actively disliked at the plant where he worked, but he was a loner. Despite that, he liked his job and hadn't been off sick for eight years.

One afternoon, he found a cat that had wandered into the plant. He picked it up so it wouldn't get caught in some of the machinery, and he put it back outside. The cat repaid his kindness by biting him on the hand as hard as it could. Jerry's boss sent him to the company doctor who gave him a tetanus shot, bandaged his hand, and put him on antibiotics. Jerry then returned to work and resumed his normal duties.

That should have been the end of it, but a couple of hours later, a loud, very human **meeooww** blared out over the intercom, echoing throughout the plant. Jerry did his best to ignore the first few meows. What else could he do?

But the meows kept coming three or four times a day for the next few days. Although Jerry's boss tried to stop it, he still found the incident amusing. Unfortunately, no one had any idea of the impending disaster.

Jerry ignored the harassment. After four days of meows, he twisted around to pick up something and a sudden sharp pain shot through his back, dropping him to the ground. After extensive testing, the doctors announced there was nothing seriously wrong with his back, just strained muscles. Unfortunately, his back never improved.

When I heard about this case, Jerry had been off work a year and a half. After the *accident,* his life went on the skids; his marriage broke up, and his back pains continued.

When I heard the story of the meows over the intercom, I understood his problem completely. Jerry clearly had a case of *Port-A-Potty Syndrome,* which I'll explain later.

I've seen many cases like Jerry's. The circumstances vary, but the underlying theme is always the same: *The individual's health fails, when he or she experiences a powerful unhappiness in life.* The source of the problem may be work, school, family life, romance, or athletics. To avoid feeling the pain, he or she tries to ignore the problem by focusing on other things, thus becoming unaware that the situation is eating away at him or her. This is a natural, normal way to respond to a difficult situation like Jerry's, but one that tends to backfire on the body.

On the surface, he caused his injury by twisting and bending, and by straining the muscles in his lower back. The fact is, however, that the strained muscles should have improved within a few days, or at most, a few weeks. The truth is that he buried the real cause of the problem —the teasing and humiliation that made him the laughingstock of the whole plant.

No matter how tough we try to be on the outside, it hurts inside. We shrug our shoulders and say, *It doesn't bother me.* But it does, whether we admit it or not. Often it develops into a powerful need to release the pressure that is building up. Jerry's hurt feelings converted into intense back pain.

## UNHAPPINESS INTO PHYSICAL SYMPTOMS

In order to understand Jerry's real problem, we need to talk about the unconscious mind. The way unhappiness converts into physical symptoms is best understood by comparing people to pressure cookers. Put a pressure cooker on the stove on high heat, and when the water comes to boil, steam builds up inside the cooker. When the pressure reaches a certain point, the little weight on top jiggles and releases some of the steam through the valve, keeping the pressure at a safe level.

Imagine what would happen if you welded the steam release valve shut and turned up the heat. When you looked at the pressure cooker on high heat, it would seem fine. It wouldn't be moving, and there would be no steam coming out. When you walked by a little later, it would look the same. Then, suddenly, without warning, KER-WHUMP!, the pot would explode.

The truth is, you are a lot like a pressure cooker. You can look and feel completely normal on the outside, yet be near bursting on the inside. Like a pressure cooker, you can handle only so much pent-up emotional steam before you explode.

When you do explode, you may either have an emotional outburst or a physical one. When you explode emotionally, you may vent on someone at work or go home and yell at your kids. When you relieve pressure by *blowing off steam,* believe it or not, you often wreak havoc on your relationships, but release enough pressure so that your frustration doesn't backfire into your body.

## THE UNSEEN PRESSURE

Sometimes, however, you can't blow off steam because you don't realize it is building up. Instead, you hide extremely powerful emotions, unknowingly, in your unconscious mind. There they build until they burst out of your body as physical pain, unbearable itching, ugly rashes, hot painful joints and other symptoms. Hurt feelings come out as physical pain. Irritation with someone comes out as itching. Feeling trapped by a situation comes out as hyperventilation and panic. Grief comes out as chest pains that bring us to tears. Anger comes out as headaches. These intense physical sensations discharge the energy of your pent-up emotions. This is one of the keys to understanding how the mind and body work together to cause illness.

## THE UNCONSCIOUS MIND

The unconscious mind is that part of the mind that holds all the memories, traumas, feelings, thoughts, and beliefs that have accumulated throughout your life. Because you can't focus attention on all this information at once, your mind stores it away from your awareness. You can access some of this stored information readily, but some of it is shielded from your conscious mind by your defense mechanisms.

For example, you may feel angry, hurt, disappointed, sad, ashamed, or humiliated, yet still be completely unaware of such feelings. Most of us experience this in one way or another. Remember when you made a Freudian slip by saying something you didn't mean to say? You may have been talking to a close friend when you suddenly exclaimed, *Why, I didn't know I felt that way about that.* The mood and time were right and suddenly the thought spontaneously emerged from your unconscious mind.

For now it's enough just to know that you have an unconscious mind and that feelings can build up in there to the bursting point. Since you are unaware of what's in there, you usually look and feel fine until your pressure cooker finally blows. Jerry's a good example of this. If anyone had asked if something was bothering him, he would have answered, *No, everything's fine.* And, he would have been telling the truth because he was completely out of touch with his feelings. Whether you like it or not, you, like everyone else, have an unconscious mind. And, like everyone else, you have feelings you are unaware of.

## WHY YOUR FEELINGS SLIP INTO THE UNCONSCIOUS

There are many reasons why your feelings slip into your unconscious. Some feelings may be too painful to keep in your conscious experience. For instance, if you experience an unhappy love affair, you may tell yourself you are over it before you really are. In Jerry's situation, most of us would have done what he did and just tried to ignore the meows, convincing ourselves that they didn't bother us.

Sometimes certain feelings may not fit into your concept of right and wrong. You may decide that since the feelings don't agree with your secular beliefs or spiritual principles, it's unacceptable to have them. As it is impossible for you to eliminate all irritation from your life, unacceptable feelings (like anger) are often stowed in your unconscious.

Other feelings are often hidden away because you were made to feel ashamed of them. Maybe your mother said, *Shame on you for talking to me that way.* From then on, those or similar feelings became painfully tinged with guilt; you may have decided it was safer not to feel anger or fear. This way of dealing with emotions often becomes a habit that persists into adulthood.

These are just a few of the reasons feelings become locked away out of sight. The various methods you use to hide feelings in your unconscious are called *defense mechanisms.* Let's look at some of them.

## KEEPING THE LID ON

Because you can only tolerate a limited amount of emotional pain, nature gave you automatic defense mechanisms with which to handle it. When the emotional pain becomes unbearable or when you just don't want to feel a certain way, the defense mechanisms take over. The three most important defense mechanisms are *minimization, denial, and suppression.*

*Minimization* works just like it sounds. You may minimize the really painful things that happen. If we ask Jerry if it bothered him that his fellow workers made fun of him, his reply would probably be: *Not really, it's not that big a deal. It bothered me in the beginning, but I'm over it now. Let them do what they want.*

In *denial* you will find you are completely unaware of the feelings that you would expect to have in a situation. Instead of feeling hurt or angry, Jerry says, *No, the meows didn't bother me.* And he means it.

In *suppression,* the feelings keep trying to come up, but you force them back by thinking about something else or by staying busy. As Jerry would say, *I don't think about the meows; I just keep busy.*

One of the main functions of your defenses is to help anesthetize you from painful events in your life. Often, you may find you simply don't know how to handle the intense emotions. You, like many others, may have grown up in families that asked you to suppress your feelings. Your only option may have been to bottle things up.

## CONNECTING SYMPTOMS TO EVENTS IN OUR LIVES

If you want to know whether some suppressed emotion is connected to a symptom — a back pain, a headache, or an aching arm — you need to ask yourself how that symptom makes you feel. Our emotional reactions to symptoms can give us valuable clues to the inner source of our problems. Does it hurt so much it makes you want to cry? Does your symptom make you feel irritable, embarrassed, or ashamed? If so, could some situation be causing that feeling?

## SOME PITFALLS

Before proceeding, there are three common pitfalls you need to consider. The first is how to deal with powerful emotional reactions. The second is blaming yourself for becoming sick. The third involves positive thinking.

## HANDLING STRONG EMOTIONS

All of us like to feel good, but unfortunately the world is an aggravating place. It's hard being married, raising kids and dealing with our parents. It's hard being part of an organization in which we have to deal with the behaviors and personalities of others.

The key to keeping these emotions from making you sick is to learn to roll with the emotional punches. That involves talking about your feelings.

Simply feeling an emotion is often enough to release its energy, but it's even better to talk about how you feel. This helps you get it out of your system. Once you face your true feelings, you will be able to free yourself from the problem. My patients are often cured during our interview, as they become aware of and talk about the feelings they have suppressed.

*Getting things off your chest* is a lot like ocean waves breaking on the shore. When a storm occurs, huge swells roll toward shore and finally break, dissipating their energy. The breaking waves actually calm the sea. Sometimes thirty-foot waves thunder in at the beach, yet just outside the breakers, the ocean is like glass. How can all that energy be discharged when the ocean beyond remains calm? The secret is that the beach offers no resistance to the breaking waves. The waves pound furiously, they roar, they send up fountains of spray. Then they expend their energy rolling up the beach.

Most of us have seen a baby or a small child become terribly upset over something, then rage or cry hysterically. These are waves of emotion breaking on the beach. Two minutes later, the child smiles and laughs. The emotions have been discharged and the child's sea of discontent is once again calm.

When thirty-foot waves come out of deep water directly into a huge cliff, they strike the cliff and rebound into the sea, colliding with the waves behind them in a chaotic, disorganized way.

This is exactly what happens when your emotions strike the barriers of your defense mechanisms and rebound into your unconscious. None of the energy can dissipate; instead, it creates a tormented state of emotional upheaval. This disease converts into physical afflictions.

## BLAMING YOURSELF

A note of caution here: It is not your fault if you have unconscious emotions that are causing pain or injury to your body. It is part of the way you are built; we all do it to one degree or another. Getting in touch with your unconscious feelings is not easy. It takes courage and often the help of a good counselor. Armed, however, with a new understanding, you can begin healing yourself.

# Positive Thinking

Often, experts tell us that all we have to do is think positively. They tell us that emotions like *anger, grief,* and *shame* are harmful to our health. They aren't. These emotions are harmful only if they are denied, minimized, or suppressed into our unconscious. There, the energy persists and builds unseen until it becomes powerful enough to wreak mischief on our bodies.

If you try to use positive thinking to avoid bad feelings, you risk pushing the feelings into your subconscious. If you permit them to surface and can work through them, in time they disappear. Joys are short-lived, and so are negative emotions, as long as you are willing to feel them and let them go.

As strange as it may seem, when you feel upset and miserable over some unhappy situation, you are reasonably safe from serious illness or injury. It is when you feel fine during these difficult periods that you are in danger. This is when your unconscious may make you sick in order to ventilate your locked-up feelings. Thus, symptoms can serve to release powerful, unconscious emotional energies.

# 2 THE UNCONSCIOUS MIND COMES TO THE RESCUE

*When you are unaware that a situation is making you unhappy, your unconscious mind may come to the rescue by giving you physical symptoms or injuries that rescue you from the situation. In order to get well, you must become aware of the problem and do something about it.*

We all have needs that we don't know about. For instance, when you lose at love, it's natural to fear risking another broken heart. This may cause you to have an inner need to avoid intimacy and bury your fears in your unconscious, where they remain hidden.

In the same vein, you may need to avoid a difficult supervisor at work, yet often keep going to work thinking, *I like my job. I'm not going to let him ruin it for me.*

Often, when you are unaware of your deeper needs, your unconscious uses your physical body to meet those needs. It almost seems to have a will of its own. It's like having someone else inside you who is in charge of your body. This *person* often creates an accident or illness, if it feels that it is in your best interest.

Specifically, it knows how to physically incapacitate you in order for you to avoid problem situations. It knows how to use symptoms and injuries to manipulate those around you, and it also knows how to use those same symptoms to get you the love and nurturing you may need. It even knows how to get you money.

In the last chapter, I talked about how Jerry's unconscious mind created his back pain, or at least intensified and prolonged it in order to release the energy of his pent-up feelings. It also removed him from his job. Since Jerry's conscious mind wouldn't take him away from his intolerable situation, his unconscious mind took over and solved the problem by creating physical symptoms.

Now let's look at another of my patients. Mary came to see me about a terrible rash on her right hand. The skin on that hand was raw, chapped, dry, and cracking. Her hand was so sore it was useless. She was right-handed and was unable to even hold a pencil. She wondered if she was allergic to pencils. I wondered if she had an unconscious need underlying the symptom. I took the usual medical history, looking for possible allergic or toxic causes. I found nothing suspicious, so I decided to interview her further.

Mary's husband owned a small business. One year earlier, he had decided that she should keep his books. Since he tended to be an overbearing dictator and wouldn't take *no* for an answer, she felt she had no choice.

To do the job, Mary had to spend two hours a day cooped up in a windowless room. That room always made her claustrophobic. She hated being under her husband's thumb. She also hated the fact that it cut into her garden time. Unfortunately, she just couldn't stand up to her husband. By the time she came to see me, she had fallen three months behind in the bookkeeping and her husband was furious. Because of his anger, she insisted I do something to make her problem go away.

When she told me how much she hated the bookkeeping, I asked her why she didn't get another job and pay a bookkeeper to keep the books. She told me she had suggested it, but her husband told her if she got an outside job, she shouldn't bother to come home.

At this point I said, *Mary, you can't do the bookkeeping because of this terrible rash. You also can't get another job without risking your marriage. What are you going to do?*

She then told me that her daughter, Jill, who had come with her to my office, had agreed to do the bookkeeping until Mary's hand improved. Subconsciously, Mary was digging in, determined to stand up to her husband even though Jill was fuming that she had to take over Mary's job.

Mary's case offers us a good example of how the dance is played out between the victim and the abuser, and of the power of physical symptoms.

This leads us to a rule: *The inability to stand up to others for our*

*rights and needs often forces our unconscious to create symptoms*
*that will manipulate people and situations to get us what we need.*

Despite my best efforts, Mary refused to consider family counseling. She couldn't see the connection between her rash and the problems with her husband. After a few uneventful visits, I referred her to a dermatologist. I imagine her rash turned out to be quite a challenge.

Having already read about Jerry's and Mary's cases, the following are a few principles to add to what you've already learned:

## When Your Symptoms Achieve Some Hidden Purpose, You Are Always Unaware That You Reap Any Benefits from the Symptoms

This is not malingering. Jerry would have been deeply insulted at the implication that his pains benefited him. Actually, he liked his work and felt the problems he had at work were relatively minor. They had nothing to do with his back pains.

## Symptoms That Our Unconscious Mind Creates Are Real, Not Imaginary

Jerry's back pains weren't imaginary; he felt like his bones were grinding together and crushing his nerves. And Mary was certainly not imagining her rash.

## When a Symptom Accomplishes Something For Us, We Need to Keep It

What would happen if Jerry's back pain went away? Then he would have to go back to work and face the same situation. That's not what his unconscious had in mind.

## When a Symptom Accomplishes Something For Us, We Become Resistant to Any Psychological Interpretation of the Problem

How would Jerry react if I told him the meows at work caused his back pain? I can just hear him saying, *Damn it, doc, I hurt my back twisting to pick something up.* Second, Jerry was busy denying that anything at work bothered him. If he admitted the back pain was related to the meows, he would have to admit that the meows really bothered him. He was emotionally unprepared to do that.

## When We Get Symptoms That Help Us, We May Have Exaggerated Emotional Reactions to These Symptoms

We often feel we need to snap at someone because of our symptoms. We can become agitated, or even hysterical. Because of the extreme pain, we don't want anyone touching the affected body part. I always know when a patient reacts that way during an examination, that powerful emotions are being released by the symptom.

In psychological circles, Jerry's suffering is commonly known as a *conversion reaction*. A conversion reaction occurs when intense emotional needs convert into real physical symptoms. The classical forms of this phenomenon often involve sudden blindness, deafness, numbness, or paralysis, all without demonstrable organic causes. What most people do not understand is the extent to which common problems such as headaches, neck and back strains, painful hands and feet, and a myriad of other problems are forms of conversion reactions.

Helpful symptoms operate in many of our illnesses, accidents, and injuries. Indeed, they are a very common way of helping us deal with problems at work, at home, in school, in sports, and in our love lives. In addition to helping us meet our needs, these symptoms demand our attention, distracting us so that we don't have to face our hidden issue. Fortunately, awareness breaks this destructive cycle. *Helpful symptoms* are essentially a sting operation conducted by our unconscious. As soon as we are aware of what is going on, the whole thing falls apart. A sting only works when everyone is fooled.

# 3 OTHER WAYS EMOTIONS AFFECT OUR BODIES

Let's look at the effects of various emotions on your physical body. *Fear,* for example, grips your body in very specific ways. Your stomach may knot up, sometimes to the point of creating stomach cramps or diarrhea. Remember the expression, *You scared the \*!#@ out of me!*

Fear acts on other organ systems as well. Your underarms sweat and produce strong smells. Your mouth often becomes dry. Your heart may race. Your hands and feet may become cold and moist. Often a speaker will say, *I'm getting cold feet about giving this presentation.*

*Anger* may cause your brow to knit, your face to flush a deep red, your muscles to tense, adrenaline to surge throughout your body, and your blood pressure to go up.

*Horror* or revulsion can take your appetite away. You may even feel nauseated or faint, as your heart slows and your blood vessels dilate.

*Grief,* another strong emotion, may make you cry. Extreme sadness can do the same thing – your eyes become red and teary, your nose stuffs up, your chest heaves, you have to clear mucus from your chest and throat, and your skin may flush bright red on your face and chest.

These are just some of the ways emotions impact your body. All emotions (even the subtle ones) are capable of causing physiological derangement, if they persist unconsciously in a magnified form and over a period of time.

This explains why so many seemingly happy people get sick. Unfortunately, our defense mechanisms often create a state of false happiness. We genuinely feel that we are happy. We don't for one minute believe that we are camped out on top of a raging sea of suppressed unhappiness, even though we often are. Here is an example of what some of these emotions can do: A young woman came to me with an irritating red rash on her upper chest and throat. The rash had made her life miserable for three weeks. Another doctor diagnosed it as poison oak and gave her cortisone pills, cortisone cream, and antihistamines. Nothing helped.

After examining her, I asked, *Wendy, what's going on in your life? Nothing, she replied. I'm moving, but I'm handling that okay.*

Even though Wendy said everything was fine, I asked her to tell me about her move anyway.

It seemed that Wendy had rented a house with another young woman two months before. They signed a year's lease together. Three weeks prior to seeing me, her roommate skipped out, leaving Wendy with the entire financial burden. She was furious, hurt, and humiliated and stuck with the first and last months' rent, and a security deposit. She also had to tell the landlord that she alone couldn't pay the rent and would have to move out.

While she explained that, she began to choke up. As she struggled to control her tears, her chest and throat suddenly flushed bright red. I told her it was okay to cry, and I asked her to look at her chest.

She looked down. The rash had flared bright red. That's when she understood that her pent-up emotions had created the problem.

Wendy's rash promptly disappeared and did not return. She had cured herself in a fifteen-minute interview by contacting and expressing her hurt feelings. In suppressing her emotions, as she had been doing prior to seeing me, she had dammed up all her physiological reactions to her intense emotions. Wendy's rash was simply her body's reaction to her suppressed feelings; her body was *trying to cry.*

Let's look at another example that involved suppressed sadness and tears. This time it caused a case of pinkeye. Surely pinkeye has nothing to do with the mind-body connection – or does it? Pinkeye (conjunctivitis) occurs when the slippery membranes lining the surface of the eye become inflamed. The common cause is germs, either viruses or bacteria, but the eye can also become inflamed by chemicals, dust, pollen, and other irritants. After treatment with medicated eye drops, it usually clears up in a few days.

Fay had gone to a clinic three weeks earlier complaining of red, irritated eyes. The doctor placed her on a sulfa antibiotic eye drop. That didn't work and a week later he switched her to a more powerful preparation, garamycin. By the time she saw me, her condition was steadily growing worse and Fay was quite concerned.

I examined Fay's eyes for evidence of infection of the cornea, signs of allergies or more serious eye conditions. I didn't find any. Her eyes were so red and inflamed, however, that it made my eyes water just to look at her. I decided to interview her and found she had recently returned to her teaching job after three months' maternity leave.

*Oh*, I said. *This condition started right after you returned to work?*

*Yes, but I like my job. Could I be allergic to something at work?*

*It's possible*, I said. *But let me ask you – was it hard to find day care for a three-month-old child? Do you have family to help?*

I could see the pain in her eyes as she answered, *No. I looked at several places. It's hard to find a good place and he's so little.* Her eyes became redder as the tears welled up. *I feel terrible every time I drop him off. I don't know if I can keep doing it.* With that, she burst into tears.

I was gratified because I knew she would now overcome her *pinkeye* problem. After she had a good cry, we talked about her options. She decided she needed to take an additional three to six months off work to take care of her baby. After this decision, her eye problem promptly cleared up.

Quite often, in my experience, pinkeye is related to our emotional lives in some way, even when germs play a role. Of course, germs can and do cause pinkeye and we need to remain open to both possibilities. When eyes are red and teary, it's good to wonder, *Are my eyes trying to cry? What might be making me sad?*

## MENTAL OR PHYSICAL?

When I conduct mind-body interaction seminars, I always receive the following questions: *Aren't there real physical illnesses that have nothing to do with mental or emotional problems? How do you tell them apart?* I admit it can be difficult, even for a doctor.

Let me give you an example: Ernie came into the office because of persistent itching, for the previous three or four weeks over his whole body. When I examined him, he had no rash, no signs of excessive scratching, no hives, and no history of breaking out in any kind of welts. He was a very hairy man, however, and his chest, arms, legs, and back were covered with a heavy growth of hair.

Somewhat puzzled, I began to search for a hidden issue. When I probed for any source of chronic, smoldering irritation, he talked freely about the fact that he was in a high-stress job. He was a record promoter, putting in long hours on the phone. As far as he could tell, nothing had changed recently, and he was a bit skeptical that his work was causing the itching, but he respected my opinion. Although I couldn't identify a definite hidden issue, I assumed his rash was emotionally caused and urged him to see a family counselor and to slow down at work.

I treated Ernie for the next three weeks with various medications, none of which helped. Then one day he came into my office with a little bottle in his hand.

*Dr. Retherford*, he said, *I was picking at the base of one of the hairs on my arm, and I found this little dark thing dug in where the hair goes into the skin. I dug it out and it has legs. It moves. What is it? I think I have them all over.*

I put it under the microscope. There, glaring at me, was a crab louse — *Pediculosis pubis*. It was squirming vigorously, obviously deeply irritated at being pinned beneath a cover slip on a microscope slide. I was so chagrined I could hardly face going back into the examining room to face him.

When I looked at Ernie's skin through a magnifying glass, I found hundreds of the little guys buried at the base of his body hairs. I explained the problem and told him that he had pubic lice all over his body. Then I apologized for missing the diagnosis and gave him some lotion to kill the infestation. The itching promptly cleared up. Despite my embarrassment, Ernie was very understanding and continued as my patient.

In my defense, crab lice are normally caught during a sexual encounter and are confined to the pubic hair. They usually don't dig in, but crawl around freely. I don't know how Ernie became infested with them in the first place, but he was so hairy that they had spread all over his body. I've spoken to many of my colleagues about this case, and none of them has ever seen a case of generalized crab lice.

When you are sick and your problem doesn't clear up, or keeps coming back, first go to the doctor for needed diagnosis and treatment, then conduct an emotional inventory to search for hidden issues. In Part III, I've included a list of questions that will help you discover if you might have hidden inner causes.

# 4 What Is My Body Saying to Me?

Consider this: Your eyes and ears sense and gather information from the world around you, your throat lets you communicate with others, and your hands help you work and play. Your back supports you and lets you do heavy work, your bladder and large intestine eliminate waste, and your sexual organs allow you to love and enjoy intimacy. In addition, your legs and feet let you walk forward to handle what lies ahead. When you face challenges in those various spheres of your life, the symptoms often affect the body parts involved. It is as if your body is a living, breathing metaphor of your inner life.

For example, if you need to block out a voice that rambles on and on, but you can't ask the person talking to stop, your ears may fill with fluid. If you hate your job, your hands may hurt. If you're angry with your lover and try to have sex, you may develop bladder or vaginal problems.

You can learn more about how emotional themes emerge in the body by listening to common American slang:

*My supervisor is so overbearing; he's a real **pain in the rear**. I wish he would **get off my back**.*

*I **can't stand** my job! It's a real **headache**.*

*I'm so disgusted at what's going on around here, I could **puke**.*

*This whole situation is **hard to swallow** – it leaves a **bad taste** in my mouth.*

*You've got to be **thick-skinned** to handle the complaints around here.*

*I am **sick and tired** of this job.*

*I don't want any more of your **foot-dragging!** Quit **bellyaching** and just do your work.*

Does our common vernacular hold an understanding and appreciation for the way our minds and bodies work together? I think it does.

Joan, a woman in her late sixties, came to me with a case of uveitis. Uveitis is an inflammation of the pigment layer of the eye, which lies next to the retina. Most often it is an inflammatory process of unknown cause. In Joan's case it had started a year before and was gradually destroying her vision. Top experts at two different university medical centers had treated it. At the time I saw her, she was on high doses of cortisone to slow down the inflammation. She was concerned not only with going blind, but also the long-term side effects of the cortisone she was taking. She was desperate, and was willing to explore the possibility of mind-body interaction.

In Joan's case, I felt the best way to explore this was to use hypnosis. She agreed. About twenty seconds after starting, she burst into tears, then began repeating over and over, *I can't stop seeing that face... I can't stop seeing that face.*

After a short time I gently asked her to tell me about the face. *It's my sister's face. It's awful — her teeth are rotting, she's all wrinkled and wasting away — just the way she looked last year when she was dying of cancer. The worst part is the horrible, accusing look,* Joan said as she burst into uncontrollable sobs. *I feel so awful about the way I let her down! Her life was so hard. She tried everything, but nothing worked. It was awful to watch her waste away. Toward the end, she didn't take care of herself or her house. Her breath smelled. She died alone when I left the hospital to go to dinner!*

Her grief poured out like a flood. All of her suppressed guilt had taken on the powerful form of her sister's dying face looking at her accusingly. To Joan, the face was saying, *You've always had it good. I've always been unhappy and miserable. Why don't you do something to make me happy? Shame on you.*

I saw Joan that one time. Then I spoke to her about four months later. The face had disappeared immediately and didn't come back. Her doctors were phasing her off cortisone because the uveitis had gone into remission. Although it left her with some residual vision loss, that was the end of the problem.

Medical textbooks do not say that uveitis is caused by chronic suppression of a highly charged, recurring, emotionally painful mental image. But in Joan's case, apparently, the chronic defensive interference with seeing *something* initiated a corresponding inflammatory process in the pigment layer of the eye.

At one time I had an on-air radio medical show. One of my callers (let's call her Louise) told me she was suffering from a terribly sore throat. An ear, nose and throat specialist suggested surgically removing her tonsils. That frightened her and she called to ask if stress might be the cause of her sore throat. I asked Louise one question, *Do you find it difficult to speak up to powerful people or superiors?*

She made an unintelligible, squeaking sound.

*What was that? A little louder, please.*

Yes, she squeaked out.

Louise gradually opened up and explained how frustrated and angry she was because she didn't have the nerve to confront certain people.

I explained that angry communications sometimes get blocked when they reach our throats (our tool for communicating with others).

If we can't express angry feelings, there is no way to resolve them. When there is no resolution, the feelings build to an intolerable crescendo. Unexpressed, painful, angry feelings can lead to a painful, angry red throat.

Before I ended my conversation with Louise, I suggested she take an assertiveness training course.

Sore throats can be caused by streptococcal and other bacterial infections, and by viral infections such as the common cold, mononucleosis, and other physical agents. Anyone who gets a sore throat is convinced they have an infection, yet 90% of throat cultures for strep are negative. The majority of sore throats I look into appear perfectly normal. The tissues are pink and healthy, with no swollen glands. Yet they hurt terribly.

Many times such sore throats are closely related to headaches. We accept that headaches are related to tension, but insist that a sore throat means we have an infection.

Juanita, a 40-year-old Hispanic woman, came to see me complaining of a month-long sore throat. Her doctor had prescribed two powerful antibiotics, which she had taken for ten days each. The first one helped a little, but the sore throat quickly returned. The second, stronger antibiotic did absolutely nothing. Her throat cultures were negative. I decided to interview Juanita through an interpreter.

She was the sole support for three children and an aging mother. Her brother had broken his leg several months earlier and had moved in with her. Since then, he had contributed nothing to the household. She was strapped for cash and fed up with his mooching, but couldn't ask him to leave.

I explained that most people recover from a broken leg in about three months. She told me that her brother had shown no signs of recovery after five months. I advised Juanita to give him two weeks to make other living arrangements. She shouldn't have to provide for him indefinitely. She took my advice and asked him to find another place to live. Later, she called to tell me her sore throat had cleared up promptly.

# 5 THE POWER OF BELIEF

I n previous chapters we've discussed four distinctly different ways in which your mind may cause symptoms in your body: (1) Your physical symptoms act as a safety valve for suppressed emotional energy. (2) Being ill or injured may produce results you don't know how to obtain any other way. (3) Unconscious emotions build up and may overstimulate your various organ systems. (4) Your unconscious *talks* to you about the realities of your life, using physical symptoms as metaphors.

To complete the picture we also need to discuss and think about the profound and sometimes stupefying effects that your beliefs can exert over your body.

For example, deeply hypnotized subjects develop a blister when touched by a pencil eraser, if they are told that it is a red-hot cigarette. This graphically illustrates the power of our beliefs over our physical bodies, a power that has been verified many times under controlled conditions by reliable investigators.

Warts can be eliminated by hypnosis, even though a virus causes them. In addition, when we deeply believe that they will go away, they do — even without the aid of hypnosis.

One little girl, for instance, had a wart that simply wouldn't go away. Her father inspected it closely, then disappeared into the bathroom. He came out with a green bottle and placed one drop of liquid from the bottle on the wart. He told her it was medicine guaranteed to cure warts. By the end of two weeks the wart had disappeared without a trace. Years later, her father told her that the *wart medicine* was a drop of plain tap water. Her deep belief cured the wart.

I also have patients who claim that an aunt or uncle can charm warts away. Some people can, others can't.

Is there really much difference between deeply believing that we are being burned by a cigarette and believing that we will hurt ourselves if we lift a heavy object? Or between believing that a wart will disappear and believing we will get sick if we go outside with wet hair? Most of us can accept the idea that our beliefs can, and often do, turn into *self-fulfilling prophecies*.

## THE ENDORPHIN REACTION

Medical researchers have discovered that our brains manufacture endorphins (powerful pain-killing substances) in response to the *idea* that we are taking a pain pill. Endorphin levels actually rise after a patient takes a placebo. And those endorphins are forty times more powerful than morphine.

That means you must be careful about what you believe. If you believe your system is strong, it will have a protective effect. Conversely, if you believe that you are susceptible to germs, you may start catching every bug that comes along.

Many people oversimplify this aspect of the mind-body connection and accept the idea that our health is simply a product of our beliefs. Like positive thinking, the theory is that if we want to get well, all we have to do is to change our beliefs. I wish that were true, but it neglects the role of the unconscious.

Remember Jerry and the cat's meow? His back pains had nothing to do with his beliefs. Jerry believed that he had a strong back right up to the point where he collapsed with pain. His back pain was related to a hidden issue. It would be a disservice to Jerry to tell him that he could get well merely by deciding that he had a strong back. That works only when you have resolved the hidden issue.

The idea of just changing beliefs to heal is like trying to make a bad-smelling mess sweet by spraying air freshener on it. You end up with a bad smell mixed with air freshener. People who are naturally healthy don't go around muttering affirmations. The experience of having good health naturally builds positive, protective beliefs.

## CONTRIBUTING TO THE PROBLEM

Unfortunately, our health-care system all too often unwittingly contributes to health problems.

Let's look at Jerry again. He had no negative beliefs about his back until he hurt himself. But the sudden deterioration of his health created a whole new set of negative beliefs. His doctors and physical therapists convinced him that he had a weak back and he had to be careful lifting. But remember, the real cause was his reaction to the meows. Once Jerry accepts that and frees himself from those false beliefs, he can recover. I have had patients with 20 years of chronic, disabling back pains who recovered completely once they understood the true source of their problem.

What about repetitive motion injuries? In the vast majority of cases, patients with such injuries suffer from a bad case of unhappiness at work. But coworkers, physical therapists and the medical profession have convinced them that repetitive motions wear them down. If that is so, why do other companies with identical workstations have no injuries?

These beliefs sweep organizations, causing epidemics of carpal tunnel syndrome, tendonitis, back strains, and similar symptoms. Job safety professionals have confessed to me that they never had a case of carpal tunnel syndrome until they posted information about it on the company bulletin board. One company manager from the San Francisco Bay Area told me that his company had a rash of back injuries right after Joe Montana, then quarterback for the San Francisco 49ers, hurt his back playing football. The company started calling it the *Joe Montana* syndrome. When people started thinking about back injuries, their backs started hurting.

The same phenomenon strikes medical students in their third and fourth years of medical school. When they begin to study various diseases, students get scared and start developing worrisome symptoms. It's a normal human reaction.

## USING WILLPOWER TO GET WELL

What happens when we make a decision to be healthy, to use our thoughts to will an illness away? Does it work?

One day on my radio show, I explained that the act of coping with difficulties through injury and disability could become a way of life.

A young woman called and said, *Doctor, you are describing me. Over the years I've had seven different injuries that forced me to go on disability. I finally realized that every one of the injuries helped me get something I needed.*

*Did you injure yourself on purpose?* I asked.

*No, I had no idea what I was doing until last year,* she said. *I had a crush on one of my bosses, but he paid no attention to me. I drove into the company parking lot one cold morning, saw him through his office window, and promptly slipped on the ice and couldn't get up. He came running out and helped me into the building. Later he accused me of doing it on purpose. I talked to a friend about it and she said, 'He's right. You literally threw yourself at him.' That really hit me. I realized I had subconsciously caused every one of my accidents to get something I needed. I decided then and there to stop it.*

*What do you mean?*

*I decided I was never going to injure myself again to get something I wanted. I've been fine ever since.*

Sometimes willpower works.

## WILLPOWER VS. HIDDEN EMOTIONS

What happens when you pit willpower against a hidden issue? Then you have a battle going on. Consciously you might say, *Darn it, I'm going to be well.* Unconsciously, your need to escape the **meows** at work is saying, *Oh yeah? I'm never going back there. Just try.* There are limits to what you can accomplish with willpower. Your desire to get well, even when very strong, can easily be overshadowed by your unconscious emotional needs.

Willpower may be extremely important, but it is never a match for a hidden issue. To use willpower effectively, you first need to understand what's happening and uncover the hidden need that is causing the problem. The key to staying well is awareness. Once you are aware of your needs and learn to take care of yourself, your decision to be well will work.

# 6 How Mind-Body Ailments Make Trouble in Our Lives

I n chapter three, I talked about how your illnesses and injuries often help you deal with your problems. However, falling back on illness or injury to get you what you need is a way of avoiding a problem. When you unwittingly fall into a pattern of chronic injuries to meet your needs, you soon find that you pay a price for coping that way – your spouse, boss, coworkers, and even your doctor may get fed up with you after a while. Let's spend a moment and look closely at how that affects you, both in the doctor's office and at home.

## SOME PROBLEMS WITH THE DOCTOR

What happens when you go to the doctor with troubling symptoms and the doctor can't find anything wrong? Imagine that you've been suffering at home for two weeks with stomach pains and have emptied your medicine chest trying every remedy you know. Nothing has helped. Finally, in desperation, you take some of your spouse's leftover antibiotics, and even those don't help. Defeated, you visit the doctor. He makes a careful examination, takes X-rays and blood tests, and then tells you everything looks okay. He hands you a bill and sends you home without giving you any medicine.

After a few days of continued suffering, you return to the doctor's office. He says, *Let's try this medicine.* You take it faithfully, but it doesn't help. By your third visit, you run the risk of being labeled as a burdensome neurotic who doesn't have anything wrong with him. Of course, even if the doctor doesn't feel that way, chances are you'll think he does. Then you start feeling guilty about taking up his time.

Finally, if you do keep coming back, the ultimate insult occurs when the doctor advises you that he thinks perhaps it's a good idea for you to see a psychiatrist.

Frequently, in this situation, our physical symptoms are coming from mind-body interactions. As patients, however, we are most often unreceptive to this idea.

How do we feel when we begin to sense that our boss, parent, spouse, or even our doctor is becoming impatient with us? For starters, we feel betrayed, insulted, hurt, and humiliated. I think that must be where the expression *adding insult to injury* comes from. It's bad enough that we are suffering pain, but when we are insulted by having our honesty doubted, it's the last straw. That is one of the most tragic things about coping with situations through illness. After a while, people start avoiding us just when we need comfort the most.

It's bad enough when it's your supervisor or your spouse, but when it's your doctor, you're in big trouble. If your doctor gets frustrated with you, or doubts that you are really in pain, it destroys the mutual trust that is vital if he is to help you recover. If you start *doctor shopping,* you risk earning a negative reputation at doctors' offices.

It is vital to break this destructive cycle. If you have been troubled by chronic or recurrent health problems, my hope is that you will open yourself to a different approach. In order to do that, however, you may have to deal with your own powerful emotional reactions.

## DEFENSIVE? WHO ME?

Experience has taught me that I must be very careful how I approach underlying emotional issues with patients, and even more careful with whom I choose to do it. While some people are grateful to me for taking time to sit down and help them with their personal problems, others resent it deeply.

Why are we so sensitive to the idea that our health problems might spring from our life experiences? The answer is rooted in society's beliefs concerning the cause of illness, as well as in our own psychological make-up. Most people expect doctors to approach them simply as physical bodies in need of repair. When we are sick, most of us go to the doctor to get fixed. We want to get our medicine and get back on the road. Doctors who talk about our personal difficulties and try to relate them to our physical symptoms make us uneasy.

Most of us believe this type of visit is a waste of time and money, because it seems like the doctor is telling us that the problem is all in our heads. When we believe that, we usually go to another doctor who concentrates only on physical explanations for our symptoms. The latter is much more satisfying and much less threatening.

What causes us to have a defensive reaction to this more holistic view of illness and injury? First is the belief that a physical symptom must have a physical cause. This is false. Second is the notion that we know how we feel. We say, *Everything is fine in my life. This is purely physical.* We forget that we have an unconscious mind and may have no idea what it is thinking.

The attitude of today's culture is that people who *have-it-together* don't have mind-body ailments. Only neurotic people make themselves sick over problems that are all in their head. That, again, is a false and destructive attitude. We all get mind-body ailments to one degree or another.

We need to change our attitudes so that we can begin to heal ourselves. Equally important is to come to grips with our defensive reactions. We need to realize that a medical problem may be helping us avoid facing some difficulty, or is helping us out of a dilemma. As long as we depend on the symptom to help us, we will be defensive when the conversation turns to our personal life.

On a brighter note, virtually all of us can make progress if we are willing to overcome our fears, look into ourselves and start unraveling our hidden issues.

# 7 Hey, I Don't Let It Bother Me

The innocent sounding title for this chapter is responsible for a tremendous amount of illness. It's one of the more common ways that we suppress feelings. While we have a choice about how we deal with our spontaneous emotional reactions, we can't control feelings. I can repeat all day until I'm blue in the face that it doesn't have to bother me if someone is mean to me. But when it happens, I had better be prepared for an emotional reaction.

In the short run, it may work to keep something from bothering us, but as we've discussed, painful feelings confined to the unconscious have a nasty habit of bursting out as physical symptoms. The following case is a graphic illustration.

Janet, a 28-year-old woman, came to see me with vaginal burning and discomfort. She and Paul had started dating six months earlier. They slept together, but did not live together. Janet wanted the relationship to become something more serious, but Paul let her know that he didn't want to get too involved.

The situation had gradually come to a head and when Janet subtly pressured him to make a commitment, he responded by not calling her anymore. It burned her up that for the previous three weeks she'd had to call him. Oh, he was very accommodating — he'd sleep with her any time she wanted.

During the week before she saw me, Janet's feelings had reached the point of crisis. Part of her felt sad to end the relationship, or at least to cool it for awhile. But a bigger part of her needed him so much that she couldn't do anything for fear of losing him. A few days before she saw me she had a bad dream in which she told him to leave her because she couldn't end it herself.

Finally she had to do something, so on Monday, three days before she saw me, she told herself she simply wasn't going to let it bother her anymore. It worked. She put it out of her mind and immediately felt better. Tuesday morning Janet woke up with a burning in her vagina. She hadn't had sex for several days and was puzzled as to why she had suddenly developed symptoms. I examined her, but apart from some mild inflammation of the tissues, everything was normal. There was no discharge and no clinical sign of infection. When I asked her if she was experiencing any unhappiness in her love life, she told me about Paul. I explained that those problems very likely had caused her vaginal symptoms.

Janet was amazed that the relationship could cause her discomfort, but as soon as she made the connection, she realized that her body was simply telling her, *It's uncomfortable to have sex with this man.*

Her case is a good example of how our bodies often don't become affected until we begin suppressing our feelings. Janet's vagina was fine as long as she could tolerate feeling her misery, but it backfired into her body when she numbed herself through an act of will by saying, *I'm not going to let this dumb relationship bother me anymore.*

Another reason some of us tell ourselves that we are *not going to let it bother me,* is because we believe that strong, healthy people simply shrug off nastiness, criticism, and insults without it affecting them. Not only do strong, healthy people *have it together* so that they don't get sick, we even believe that they don't even get bothered or upset. The notion that if we become upset, obviously we are emotionally incompetent boobs, is false. It's normal and healthy to be bothered by things.

It's okay to acknowledge feeling hurt or angry at the way you're being treated. This stage lasts hours, days, or even weeks, depending on the degree of upset. It helps to talk about your feelings. After an appropriate amount of time, you may say to yourself, *Now, I'm going to take a deep breath and try to let it go. I'm going to try to understand why this person is acting this way and do my best to forgive him.* Then notice if it worked – or whether you still feel angry and hurt. If the feeling persists, keep working at it. This is a healthier way of dealing with your feelings than proclaiming, *I'm not going to let it bother me.*

## How Our Upbringing Teaches Us to Suppress Our Feelings

Most of those who tell themselves that they're not going to let things bother them are systematically (but unintentionally) trained to do so by their parents.

Tony was sent by his parents to see me because he was developing a *negative attitude* in school and his grades were suffering. I noticed that, like most teenagers, he tended to be rather noncommittal about his feelings. In talking about problems at school, he said, *I don't have to let that bother me.*

So I asked, *Well, how would you feel about that situation, if you did let it bother you?*

*I don't let those kinds of things get to me.*

*How can it not get to you? It would really bother me a lot.*

As we talked, it was beautiful to watch the boy open up and start to pour out his feelings. All he had needed was someone to tell him that feelings were okay. His problem involved two or three guys on the swimming team who were razzing him. It turned out that whenever Tony attempted to talk to his parents about that or other school problems, they would tell him he didn't need to let it bother him. It hurt them to see Tony in pain, so they tried to help in the only way they knew how, by teaching him to be *tough* and deny the hurt. They didn't know that all he needed was someone to listen to him and to validate his feelings. Tony quickly made a complete recovery, his concentration returned to normal, and he started making good grades again.

---

Being strong isn't about not having hurt feelings; rather, it's about learning to tolerate and express those feelings. Unfortunately, it becomes more difficult to tolerate our emotions if we can't talk about them to anyone.

Our society doesn't do a good job of preparing us to deal with negative feelings like fear, anger, hurt and shame. We're told we have to learn to control our emotions, but we're not taught how to do it. Powerful emotions, like all things, have a season. When they are expressed to an understanding friend, they tend to evaporate and pass away without any effort. It relieves us and makes us feel good when a friend listens to our frightened or hurt feelings and says, *I've felt that way, too.* When we cannot bring ourselves to express the feelings to another person, they tend to hang around. But in time they all pass if we are able to feel them consciously.

It's not too surprising then, that after a few doses of that medicine, a child begins to disapprove of himself when he experiences intense negative emotions. Then he begins to keep his tender feelings to himself and attempts to appear invulnerable to his parents and the rest of the world in order to gain their approval. Or worse, in time he becomes completely unconscious of those hurt, tender feelings because he can't tolerate the shame attached to them.

# Section II

# Common Situations That Make Us Sick

# 8 Raw Deal Syndrome, Friday Night Fever & Schoolitis

## Raw Deal Syndrome

*Raw Deal Syndrome* is about resentment. We may resent our government, our spouse, our neighbor, our attorney, our doctor, or our in-laws. Most of the time, however, *Raw Deal Syndrome* concerns our resentments about our work. As adults, much of our happiness and unhappiness revolves around how satisfying we find our jobs.

Job satisfaction depends on two things: how much we enjoy our work and how the company or our fellow workers treat us. When we become unhappy at work, illness or injury may follow.

Think back to a time when you were unhappy at work. You might have been a victim of your boss's favoritism toward a co-worker. Or someone else took credit for your idea. Or you suggested a way to do your job better or more efficiently, and your superiors didn't adopt it. Maybe your boss told you to do something you'd opposed, even though you had a legitimate objection.

Feeling resentful over things like that is a normal, natural human reaction.

Sally, a supermarket bagger, came to see me about a back pain that started just after she had lifted a couple of fifty-pound bags of rock salt. The examination and X-rays were negative. Because her symptoms were mild, I gave her medication and released her to go back to work. When she returned in five days, she complained that her back was worse. She also reluctantly admitted that she had slammed her arm in a customer's car door earlier that day.

She was a small woman, so common sense told me she might strain her back lifting fifty-pound sacks, and it could be a coincidence that she had injured herself twice in five days despite the fact she hadn't had an injury during the previous three or four years. But her worsening pain, combined with the second injury, made me believe she had a hidden issue.

I sat down with Sally and asked if she was unhappy about anything at work. She raised her eyebrows and began to tell me about some work problems. Six months before, she had reported the store's assistant manager for sexual harassment. Even after she reported him, he had continued to bother her. *I'm married*, she told him. *What difference does that make?* he asked, and continued to press her.

She put up with it as long as she could, then reported him again. The store fired the assistant manager and that resolved the situation.

Unfortunately, over the last two or three weeks, several of the other baggers started disappearing into the storeroom, leaving Sally to do most of the work. When she confronted them, they shrugged it off.

Sally knew her manager liked her, but she was reluctant to go to him again for fear of being labeled a chronic complainer. She was stuck. Enter her back injury. When I sent her back to work, her unconscious upped the ante by increasing her back pain and by getting her elbow slammed in the door to boot. Sound silly? Such *accidents* are actually common.

After I talked to her, she realized how much the situation was bothering her and talked to her manager about the new problem. As soon as she faced it, her *accident-proneness* and back pains went away. As doctors, we are trained to take a careful medical history from every sick or injured person we see. This includes a history of the present illness. We record when and how the problem started, as well as past medical history. In Sally's case I asked how heavy the bags of rock salt were, whether she was accustomed to lifting heavy objects, where the pain was, and so on. The history included whether she had ever injured her back before, whether she had any inherited conditions that might affect her back, and whether she was on any medications.

In this case, those things had almost nothing to do with Sally's real problem. In reality, the significant past history had to do with the complaint about the sexual harassment, getting the assistant manager fired, and about her reluctance to make waves. Her lazy coworkers caused her present illness.

In the context of standard medical treatment, such things are completely hidden and never addressed. It's no wonder work-related injuries so often seem to go on and on forever.

———⟫-०-⟪———

A similar case of *Raw Deal Syndrome* involved Bob, a truck mechanic who worked for a small trucking firm. Bob and another mechanic maintained the company trucks. Both felt overworked. There was a lot of work and their employer always expected them to put in overtime, which he also always seemed to worm his way out of paying for. Bob and his partner requested more help, but nothing happened. Finally, his partner quit in disgust. Because this left Bob to do all the work alone, his morale dipped to a low ebb.

He expected the owner to replace his partner, but nothing happened. Bob felt totally used, abused, disgusted, and angry, and finally started looking for another job. The day before I saw him, he'd received an offer to go to work for another company, starting in two weeks.

That day he put in his usual ten hours and left, locking the outside gate. As he turned the key in the padlock, an excruciating pain shot through his lower back and dropped him to the ground. The pain brought tears to his eyes.

When he reached my office he was in great pain. His X-rays were normal. All I could find were muscle spasms and limited mobility due to the severe pain. I put him on painkillers and muscle relaxants and took him off work. Despite my best efforts, the pain kept him away from the job for the next two weeks. At the end of that time, he'd recovered enough to start the new job. During the first few days on the new job, the pains disappeared completely.

Notice the symbolism of the onset of pain; it occurred when he turned the key to lock the gate at the end of the day's work. Bob didn't know it, but his collapse and excruciating pain at that moment were caused by his unconscious decision to not go to work another day for *that jerk.*

Sometimes, when people have injuries like that, employers and doctors tend to think they are faking it. Ask yourself these questions:

Did Sally fake her back pains and slam her elbow in the car door on purpose? Did Bob fake his back pain and tears to collect disability? People who are naive about the way their unconscious uses their bodies to extricate them from problem situations might think so, but they would be wrong. Sally and Bob's pains were real. They were simply related to their hidden issues.

I have treated hundreds of cases of *Raw Deal Syndrome*. The most common way *Raw Deal Syndrome* expresses itself is as the common low-back strain. In fact, smoldering resentment is the most common cause of low-back pain. When I search for hidden issues in people whose backs are injured at work, I nearly always find resentment.

Are all back problems emotionally induced? Of course not. We can physically strain our back muscles or rupture a disc by bending or lifting. We can break bones in our spine, contract cancer of the spinal cord or vertebrae, break our ribs, and have kidney stones. But low-back strain is often a catch-all for those patients whose backs hurt, but who have no evidence of organic disease. It's significant that the vast majority of such patients were injured at work and are out on worker's compensation. Most of the cases result from injured feelings and pent-up aggravation, rather than genuine physical injury, although the pains are real.

*Raw Deal Syndrome*, with its brooding bitterness, doesn't just cause low-back pain; it can also manifest itself as pain in our hands, wrists and shoulders.

## FRIDAY NIGHT FEVER

Often I have patients who are frightened over the way their symptoms come and go, seemingly without explanation.

It is not unusual for a person with a back strain to leave their doctor's office on Monday in great pain, improve to almost 100 percent over the next two or three days, then suddenly relapse without warning the day before their next doctor's visit. What's going on here? The person could be lying to get the doctor to take him or her off work, which occasionally happens. But most of the time their pain is real and disabling. It is simply occurring on an "as needed" basis. The unconscious knows that there better be pain, otherwise the doctor will return the patient to work where his or her hidden issue lurks.

This behavior is two-fold because the person with this syndrome is unaware of it. He or she is also unaware of why employers are so infuriated. Visualize this: The doctor encourages the patient to resume normal activities as pain allows, so the patient decides to go dancing Friday night to test his back. After all, he's now feeling fine and can stop right away if it bothers him. So he dances and everything's okay. However, one of his bosses sees him dancing. The next afternoon he gets up off the couch from watching football and his back goes out. He regrets dancing and thinks it must have caused his relapse. He doesn't realize he is suffering from *Friday Night Fever.*

Monday morning, I get an angry call from the employee's boss advising me that my patient, who was supposedly disabled with a back injury, was spotted Friday night winning the Western dance competition at the local night spot. (This situation actually happened.)

Although the patient may occasionally fake it, usually he or she is not. Unfortunately, the symptoms come and go on an as needed basis, which is something employers have a hard time understanding.

When people are injured at work and the boss suspects malingering, three things need to happen: The employer needs to put the employee back to work on a limited basis, try to discover the employee's possible hidden issue, and then take steps to resolve it. In the real world, this almost never happens. The employer usually doesn't want to talk to his worker, because he is convinced that he or she is faking it. The employer, at that point, feels totally negative about the employee. (Often the employer felt totally negative about the person before the injury and regarded him or her as a problem. Many times this is an important piece of the hidden issue.) The worker senses his boss's dislike and gets injured in order to escape a painful situation. Unfortunately, some employers don't feel comfortable talking about problems with employees. They are not good at it, they feel the employee is impossible, or they don't have time. Further, such employers may say they are there to run a business, not to baby-sit whining workers. The employee, of course, usually won't take the problem to the boss, but does his best to ignore it.

My attempts to resolve hidden issues between employees and managers are usually a dismal flop. Most often, the employer feels he has already done as much as he can. I have, however, seen some notable exceptions. Once managers are trained to understand the role of hidden issues, they often cooperate in resolving the problem.

Symptoms like sore throats or coughs, which come and go mysteriously over a period of several weeks, are often a form of *Friday
Night Fever*. They can be related to difficulties you may encounter
in any sphere of your life. Just look for what they help you avoid in
order to zero in on the problem.

### SCHOOLITIS

*Friday Night Fever* doesn't happen only to adults. It also happens
to kids who have to go to school on Monday morning. After all, that
is their workplace. For example, if your child becomes ill on the
weekend, there is a possibility that he or she is having difficulty
facing something that is coming up in school during the coming week.

Jenny, a 12 year old, came to see me Sunday afternoon. The day
before, she suddenly came down with a stuffy nose and cough. Her
symptoms became worse and by Sunday she was running a 101-
degree fever. Jenny and her mother were puzzled, because Jenny
was rarely sick and the symptoms appeared out of the blue. Jenny
said, *Mom, I don't think I am going to be able to go to school tomorrow.
I feel really sick.*

I casually asked Jenny how school was going. After she told me
everything was okay, I asked if she had anything big coming up.

*I have to do a book report and I'm only three-quarters of the way
through the book,* she said. *It's due Tuesday. The really big thing,
though, is that I was supposed to turn in the outline for my science
project last week. I haven't, because I can't figure out what to do.
The final outline is due the day after tomorrow. I had the same
problem last year.*

Clearly, she was feeling overwhelmed. After leaving the office, her
mother sat down and helped her decide on her science project topic.
While she was home sick Monday, they outlined it together. By dinner-
time Monday, Jenny had made a miraculous recovery. If she hadn't
received the help, however, her illness might have dragged on for
days or weeks.

⟜➤•◀⟞

Let me give you another example: Johnny's mom brought him to
my office because he had complained about stomach pains. Like

Jenny, Johnny never complained of illness, so his mother was concerned that he might have appendicitis.

I examined him and found no signs of any serious problems. I told his mother that his stomach pains most likely were caused by contractions of the intestines. I explained that the condition is called irritable bowel syndrome, that it is one of the most common causes of stomach pains in children and that it is often caused by some unhappiness at school.

*Johnny's not having any problems at school, she told me defensively. He's an excellent student and has lots of friends.*

I turned to him. *Johnny, is anybody calling you names at school? He burst into tears. Yeah, Martin's been calling me stupid. He keeps doing it.*

His mother looked astonished. She put her arms around her son and asked, *Honey, why didn't you tell me?*

It's important to know that children usually keep their problems to themselves. The next day, Johnny's mother went to the teacher and explained the problem. Martin stopped teasing Johnny and the stomach pains stopped almost immediately.

Children can be well-adjusted students and still go through painful situations with teachers or other children. The problem may relate to a power struggle with a teacher, falling behind in school-work, a subject they hate, discomfort with physical education, or anticipating team tryouts or play auditions.

---

Let's look at a case that involves school sports. Timmy's mother brought him in with a sprained ankle. Both parent and child were concerned about the upcoming pitching tryouts for Little League.

Some families get very involved in Little League and become extremely competitive. Timmy's father had spent a lot of time helping his son with his pitching to prepare him for the tryouts. The boy had pitched for the team the previous year and the family hoped he'd be the star pitcher this time around. Apparently it was not okay to talk about feelings in that family, because when I mentioned that I'd be nervous about the tryouts, both he and his mother denied that he had any such feelings.

On the outside, Timmy had convinced himself that he would do great. Inside, it was too much pressure. He ended up having to miss the tryouts because his ankle hurt too much. It took a while, but the family finally accepted that and let Timmy handle it in his own way.

—————➤◆◀—————

Overweight teenage girls often struggle with their physical education teachers over running. In one case, the girls had to run a mile around the track, and the teacher threatened to flunk them if they didn't try harder.

Children like these often show up in my office with knee pains that prevent them from running. The parents are usually frustrated and angry with the teacher and want a note from the doctor to excuse the child from running. X-rays and examination are normal in most of these cases, yet there is some disabling pain. We are always quick to jump to a physical explanation for pain, but we need to also consider the possibility that it has a purely emotional cause. In this case the unconscious knows exactly how to defeat that P.E. teacher: a knee that hurts so much that walking, much less running, is out of the question. Such injuries could easily be prevented if physical education teachers would offer alternative forms of exercise for children who have problems with running.

If your children have problems that prevent them from going to school or participating in some school activity, you should remember to ask if there is some problem at school that is troubling them. The questions need to be specific: *Is anyone calling you names? Are you behind in any of your schoolwork? Has anyone threatened you?* Often, once you uncover the cause, the physical symptom disappears.

# 9 ACCIDENTALLY ON PURPOSE

Sometimes things happen to us that are outside our control. Earlier I talked about Sally, the grocery bagger, slamming her arm in a customer's car door, as if it was somehow caused by her need to avoid work. For those of you who are understandably doubtful that our unconscious is capable of engineering accidents, I'd like to tell you about Rosie.

Rosie was involved in a car accident on a rainy night. Coming up too fast behind a big truck, she slammed on the brakes and skidded out of control. Although she didn't hit the truck, she was so badly shaken that the highway patrol officer at the scene suggested she go to the emergency room. The doctor there told her that her X-rays were normal. She had no serious injuries, yet she complained of neck and lower-back pains. Her diagnoses were neck and lower-back strains.

Despite her protests that she wanted to return to her job, Rosie's back and neck improved slowly. When her injuries began to get better, she developed uncomfortable sensations down her leg and a numb, tingly feeling in the left side of her face and left arm. Even worse, she started to lose her voice. For a period of about four months, she could speak only in a whisper. The diagnosis by the expert was dysphonia, malfunction of the vocal cords of unknown cause.

After months of speech therapy and supportive counseling, the following scenario gradually came to light. Rosie worked in her husband's family business. Not long before her accident, her husband's sister had come to work in their store. The family had sold their other shop, leaving no other place for the sister-in-law to work. This tightly knit family felt they had to make a place for her.

Rosie and her sister-in-law didn't get along. But the newcomer was family, so she was put in charge of ordering merchandise, which was formerly part of Rosie's job (the part Rosie enjoyed most). Rosie couldn't speak up and confront the situation head-on. She told her husband that she didn't like his sister and didn't want her in the store. The husband said he couldn't ask the family to fire her. He understood that the sister was abrasive and difficult to get along with, and that she had usurped part of Rosie's job, but he was caught in the middle. Rosie was stuck. After that, the tension began to mount, right up to the day she had her car accident.

This is where the story gets even more interesting. After being out of work for six months, she got better and started to think about returning to work. We had talked at length about her situation, but she still had not been able to bring herself to talk to her sister-in-law about her feelings.

The day before she was to return to work, she had another car accident. She was hospitalized with minor injuries and couldn't return to work for several more weeks. As Rosie's case demonstrates, when we're in a situation that makes us intolerably uncomfortable inside, but we can't – or won't – get ourselves out of it, our unconscious often arranges some incapacitating accident or injury for us.

Can our unconscious really do that? The answer is yes. I have seen it happen over and over again. Our need to avoid certain situations is so powerful at times that it seems to extend out around us in a web. Accidents often befall us that don't seem to be our fault. We may crash into cars that suddenly swerve in front of us. We think of these things as *accidents*. Sometimes, however, *accidents* happen when we desperately need to avoid something.

Of course, real accidents happen. Airplanes crash, trains jump their tracks, drunken drivers slam into innocent people, and earthquakes occur. Hidden issues are the driving force in some accidents and play no part whatsoever in others.

You may think cases like Rosie's are rare, but they are quite common. In fact, people can end up even worse off than Rosie, with severe, disabling injuries, as we will see in Leonard's case.

Leonard had reached a critical point in his marriage and couldn't understand why he had married his wife. They were, he felt, exact opposites. He liked to socialize, she didn't. He liked to talk about his feelings, and she clammed up about things that bothered her. He liked one church and she liked another. Even worse, he felt that she had caused him to give up all his close friends, while she maintained hers. When another woman, Linda, came along, he fell in love with her. Linda was equally in love with him, and pressured him to divorce his wife and marry her.

That was not to be. As unhappy as Leonard was in his marriage, he couldn't bear the thought of hurting his wife. He found himself in one of those no-win situations where he was damned if he did, and damned if he didn't. The thought of staying was unbearably painful, but so was the thought of leaving.

His unconscious solved the conundrum in a most creative fashion. A truck suddenly swerved into Leonard's lane and collided with his car head-on at high speed. He suffered numerous broken bones and spent months in the hospital. Things came to a head when Linda ran into his family at the hospital. You can imagine how the sparks flew. He couldn't ask his wife and children to stop visiting him, so he felt forced by circumstances to tell Linda not to visit him any more.

Both women gave him an ultimatum: choose me or her. That was exactly what Leonard had not been able to do before. But his injuries and dependency tipped the scales and forced him to choose his wife. Is it possible that his deeper parts somehow arranged to incapacitate him in an attempt to resolve the unbearably painful situation? Could they have somehow caused his car accident? I believe they did.

Leonard's injuries affected his pelvis and kept him from having sexual relations with anyone. Was this just a coincidence? I think not.

⟹•◦•⟸

Sylvia, a college student, was in a live-in relationship that was going stale when she began seeing someone else on a casual basis. Both men were in love with her and her casual lover, Brent, was pressuring her to leave her live-in boyfriend and move in with him. The day before she hurt herself, she had been on the phone with Brent. In a moment of weakness, she agreed to stop by his place the next day on her way home from class, to give him her answer.

The next morning she got on her bicycle, just as she had done hundreds of times before, turned onto the street at the bottom of her driveway and skidded on a patch of loose gravel. She landed on her tailbone, which hurt so much she could hardly walk.

Fortunately, nothing was broken. The doctor said she had just bruised her tailbone. All Sylvia knew was that it hurt so much that sex was out of the question for several weeks.

Her injury cooled her involvement with both men. Ultimately, she broke up with both and moved into her own place. The bottom line was that she was not ready to get involved in a committed relationship with anyone.

Interestingly, Sylvia told me that now any time she feels pressured by a man, her pelvis hurts. Recently, a male friend called to invite her over to his place to *trade massages*. She couldn't decide what to do until she suddenly got a sharp pain in her pelvis. She told him no. What she learned is that when she *can't say no,* her pelvis will say it for her.

---

So far we've discussed a car accident and a bike accident. Let's look at a construction accident that served a similar function.

Henry, a contractor, was building a house for a private party. His client had agreed that the construction would be accomplished in four stages and that he would be paid at the completion of each stage. In addition, it was agreed that if he completed any stage ahead of schedule, he would receive a bonus.

Things began to go sour between Henry and his client shortly after the project started. The first inkling he had that his client might not keep his word came when Henry spent several hundred dollars of his own money on a transit they needed to lay out the foundation. They agreed to split the cost fifty-fifty.

Henry was never reimbursed and this incident started a sequence of events that led to his injury. It was the first insult. Several others followed, the biggest being that his bonuses were delayed, and when they did arrive, were several thousand dollars less than had been agreed upon.

The longer the job went on, the more the wrongs festered. Finally, Henry got to the point where he hated going to work and didn't really want to be there at all. But he felt he had to finish the job, so he continued working on the project.

During this period, Henry got married and took two weeks off for his honeymoon. His first hour back on the job, he was climbing around the second story and stepped on a board that wasn't nailed down. He fell fifteen feet to the ground and broke his back and pelvis. His injuries damaged the nerves to his bladder and legs. He wound up in a full-body cast and had to have corrective surgery on his spine.

When I saw him, he was still filled with unresolved anger toward his client. I felt he needed to resolve those feelings for his own sake. He needed to work through and drop his resentments toward the man, clearing the way for his complete recovery, if that was possible.

Needless to say, Henry didn't have to return to the job, since he was physically incapacitated for six months. His client had to hire another contractor.

From my perspective, it was not a coincidence that his accident happened just as he was going back to a job he hated, working for a man who was systematically cheating him. At a deep level, Henry simply didn't want to be there any more, yet he couldn't see his way clear to quit. Thus his unconscious disabled him.

The solutions that our unconscious comes up with are nearly always effective at meeting our deepest needs, but they are often frightening in their intensity. The unconscious can easily cause great pain and disability, extracting us from our problems. I feel confident that if Henry had confronted his client about the issues and had worked it out or quit the job, the accident would not have happened.

What's the moral of this story? If we stay in a situation we hate, we run the risk of serious injury. If we can't resolve our resentments or get ourselves out of the situation, our unconscious may remove us from it. If we do stay in the situation, at the very least we should ventilate our feelings about it with a therapist once a week until we are through it, and we should make a conscious decision that we are not going to injure ourselves to escape it.

## TAKE ME OUT OF THE BALL GAME

*Accidents* happen to athletes, too.

My patient Brian had taken up surfing a few years earlier. He fell in love with the sport and it became his goal to surf the big waves of the great winter surf at Sunset Beach in Hawaii.

There was only one problem with surfing those waves: people drown doing it. Four- to six-foot waves are fun, ten- to twenty-foot waves are scary, and twenty- to thirty-foot waves make the average person terrified.

But Brian didn't want to admit he was afraid. If he let his fear come up, he might have second thoughts about the surf.

Did he make it to Hawaii to surf the big waves? I suppose he might have, if he'd had a chance to talk about his fears with someone before he went. As it was, I didn't see Brian until after his skiing accident two weeks before his trip to Hawaii. He broke his leg so severely it left him with a permanent limp. The injury forced him to abandon the idea of surfing the waves at Sunset Beach.

You might wonder what kinds of fears of injury, failure, or humiliation athletes go through. It varies, but almost everyone has at least some butterflies before a competition.

The best form of prevention is to talk about your fears. Talking about the feelings and even just admitting them to yourself will help prevent them from backfiring into your body as injuries. The ability to face the *agony of defeat* is an integral part of any successful athlete's make-up.

People talk about how important it is to visualize success, and how damaging it is to hold negative thoughts or fears. The implication is that we must ignore or stamp out any fears we have so they won't interfere with our performance. This ignores the fact that fears and doubts are normal occurrences and that there are right ways and wrong ways of dealing with them.

It is important and necessary to visualize success in order to do well. But if that is simply layered on top of powerful, unconscious dread, it will never work.

⟹•◦•⟸

Sharing our innermost fears is not easy. It has to be done with someone we feel comfortable with. Someone who can listen and understand. Most of the time when we try to share with our families and friends, they say something like, *No, don't think that way. Think positive.* This type of response just makes us clam up and feel worse.

What we really need to hear is, *Yeah, I'd feel the same way going into a situation like that.*

Just as common as accidents and injuries are mysterious aches and pains that appear prior to competition – pains that don't seem to be related to any injury. Those can be equally effective in sidelining us. Tom came into the emergency room after an auto accident. The ambulance personnel brought him in strapped to a full-body back-board because he was completely paralyzed from the waist down. The board was needed to immobilize his neck and spine to prevent further injury to his spinal cord.

I was a bit surprised that Tom apparently had suffered a grave spinal cord injury, because the car was only going about ten or fifteen miles per hour at the time of the accident. The car stopped, he fell out the back door and ended up without a mark on him.

As I began to evaluate him, the first words out of his mouth were, *You gotta get me better doc, because I'm flying to Vegas next week to compete in a nationally televised martial arts match.* His urgency about it immediately made me suspect a hidden issue was involved.

I examined him, and sure enough, he couldn't move his legs or feet, or even wiggle a toe. I took out a sharp needle and poked him from his hip to his toes. He felt nothing. For medical reasons that I won't go into here, I suspected that the numbness and paralysis might be psychological in origin, rather than a spinal injury.

*Tom,* I said, *tell me about this martial arts meet that is coming up next week.*

*I'm going to Vegas and I'm going up against Chuck Norris,* he replied.

*I guess you must be pretty good to go up against someone like him. Aren't you nervous?*

*No, I'm going to kick his butt.*

That took me a back a bit, so I asked, *How can you be sure? Have you ever fought him before?*

Reluctantly, *he said, Yeah, he whipped me bad. But that's not going to happen this time.*

*If I were you,* I said, *I'd be at least a little nervous. Aren't you worried about it?*

*No, I'm not. I told you, I'm taking him this time. I've been training hard.*

*Well,* I said, *I want you to do one thing for me. I want you to think about how it would make you feel if you fought him next week, and there on national TV he whipped you again in front of the world.*

Finally, after a pause, Tom said, *That would be totally humiliating.* At that point I asked the nurses to take him over to X-ray and have his neck and back examined. When he was wheeled back forty-five minutes later, his numbness and paralysis had disappeared. I told him that his X-rays were normal, and as long as he didn't have any further symptoms, it was okay if he competed in Vegas. I wished him luck.

Once Tom had consciously acknowledged to another person his fear of humiliation, it became more tolerable. Remember: *When you face fear, it always becomes less frightening.* His unconscious decided that it was all right to proceed and gave him back the use of his legs.

He put on his clothes and walked out of the emergency room. I never heard what happened in his match against Chuck Norris.

# 10 You've Gotta Get Me Better, Doc, Because...

When a symptom prevents us from doing something important, naturally we go to the doctor. Often, the first thing we say is, *Doctor, you've got to get me better, because I've got to fly to the coast next week, and I can't go if this foot keeps hurting... I must go back to work because this is the busiest time of the year and two people are off on vacation... You've got to get me over this laryngitis. I have to give a speech tomorrow...*

Such complaints always alert me to the possibility that the subconscious may have taken over to prevent the person from doing something he or she may want to do, but is dreading inside. The patient, however, almost never relates the symptoms to the up-coming event.

As a doctor, the challenge for me when a patient says, *You've got to get me better doctor,* is to gently make the patient aware of the polarity of his or her feelings. I know that once the patient gets in touch with the unacknowledged dread, the symptoms will frequently disappear. Let's look at an example.

Gwen, a woman in her forties, hopped into my office one Monday morning on one foot and told me that her foot was killing her, and I had to get her better by Sunday night because she was going hiking in the Grand Canyon. Obviously, she wasn't going anywhere if we couldn't get her foot back in commission.

I asked the usual questions: *Had she fallen and twisted her foot? Dropped something on it? Strained it in an aerobics class?* She said no to everything. It had started earlier that day and had become extremely painful. I took some X-rays. There were no stress fractures, bone cysts, tumors, or other problems. Her foot appeared normal.

After telling her I couldn't find any physical problem, I asked how she felt about hiking in the Grand Canyon. *I'm looking forward to it,* she said. *But my foot really hurts.*

*I'm sure it really hurts,* I said. *And I'm also sure you want to go on the trip. But, think, is there anything frightening you about this particular trip?*

*No, I really want to go. Well, maybe the heat.*

*The heat?*

*Gwen's hand went to her mouth with a sharp intake of breath. Could that be it?*

*What happened?* I asked.

*About four years ago, while traveling in Italy, I collapsed from the heat. The next thing I knew, people jabbering in Italian were loading me into an ambulance. I thought I was dying. I've never felt so awful, and I was terrified. Later, in the hospital, an interpreter told me I had heat stroke, but that I would be fine.*

I asked, *Gwen, have you heard the stories about people collapsing from heat in the Grand Canyon and having to be carried out on mules?*

She nodded dumbly.

*Do you think maybe your unconscious is trying to make sure you don't get another case of heat stroke?*

*Could that make my foot hurt like this?*

*Yes.*

*Is there anything I can do? I really want to go on the trip.*

*I want you to go home and tell your husband that you are worried about the heat, especially after your problem in Italy. Second, I want you to call the park ranger at the Grand Canyon and explain that you have had problems with heat in the past. Ask if he thinks it's safe for you to go down to the bottom this time of year. Ask him what the heat is like now and what precautions you should take.*

Clutching her bottle of pain pills, Gwen hopped out of the office. Two weeks later, I received a post card from Phantom Ranch, at the very bottom of the Grand Canyon. It read, *Thanks to you, Dr. Retherford, every bone in my body is aching from the hike, but my foot doesn't bother me a bit.*

It was nice to have a happy ending.

————►◦◄————

In Gwen's case, her dread of the heat was completely unconscious. Even if I had known about her heat stroke and asked how she felt about it, she would undoubtedly have said she hadn't thought about it in years.

How can you harbor a fear powerful enough to cause a real, incapacitating pain, yet be completely unaware of it consciously? One of the ways you may deal with the traumatic events in your life is by forgetting about them – it's normal. Most people, however, don't realize that there are two ways to *forget* a trauma: You can process the trauma internally by suppressing it. When you do, powerful feelings of fear, hurt, horror, or revulsion are submerged into your unconscious, where they lurk as icebergs, waiting just below the surface.

You can fully acknowledge your feelings and talk about them with a friend or counselor. When you do that, the trauma gradually loses its sting and you can forget it without leaving an iceberg behind.

## More Mysterious Foot Pain

Josie came into the office with excruciating foot pain. The pain was mysterious, however, because – as far as she was concerned – she had done nothing to injure herself. The X-rays and examination were completely negative.

I didn't know Josie, but I suspected she must have been dreading something. I asked if she had a trip planned in the near future. She did. She told me that she was married to Al, who came from a large Puerto Rican family. Each year she and Al stayed with his parents in another state. All his brothers, sisters, and cousins lived in the neighborhood and were in and out of the house all the time.

Her family was due to leave the following week for a two-week stay with Al's parents. Josie told me that her foot had better stop hurting because she couldn't bear the trip if the pain continued.

Her dread was pretty close to the surface. She felt she had an obligation to take the trip once a year, so Al's parents could see the grandchildren and visit with their son. They were nice people, but the entire atmosphere surrounding the visit bothered her.

Her mother-in-law served nothing but beans. While at home, Josie insisted her children have salads and green vegetables. Worse, her husband's family didn't value higher education, particularly for girls. The men were all macho and the women were supposed to kowtow to them. Over the years, she had let her husband know, in no uncertain terms, that he couldn't treat her or their daughter that way. He had gradually come to accept this, but he regressed to his old ways when he visited his family. Josie was especially terrified that her daughter would follow the example of the other girls in her husband's family; namely, become pregnant and marry at fourteen.

The men in the family resented Josie and told Al that he shouldn't tolerate her behavior. She had thought about sending him there alone, but they had four nonrefundable airline tickets. Still, she couldn't stand the idea of going.

Opening up to me and ventilating her conflicting feelings was the start of Josie's cure. I validated her feelings and agreed that it was a difficult situation for her and she had every right to dread the trip. As we talked, she realized she also had the right to buy vegetables for herself and her children. It was also okay for her family to get out of Al's parents' house and go somewhere else for a few days, and it was acceptable for her to rent a car, so she wouldn't be stranded in the house twenty-four hours a day, while Al went off with the boys.

If the visits continued to be difficult for her, they could be shortened to a week at a time and made every two years, instead of every year. Next time, she could also insist that Al's parents come to her house. I explained that she was not being selfish by standing up for her needs.

When she left my office, Josie felt more comfortable about the trip. I explained to her that she could probably expect her foot pain to diminish, as her concerns about the trip decreased. This proved to be true. She followed my advice and gave herself permission to buy her children vegetables and to get away for a short time during the visit. The result was that her pain vanished completely.

## If Your Feet Don't Stop You,
## Your Knees Will

The previous two cases involved pain without any physical signs of injury or inflammation. Can dread cause pain with real physical symptoms? Let me introduce you to Margaret.

Margaret's husband, a peace officer, won a trip for two to Russia. Three weeks before the trip, Margaret came to me with the familiar request, *You've got to get me better, doc, because... I'm going abroad in three weeks, and I have to be able to walk.*

Her right knee was not only painful and tender, but it was also red, hot and swollen. Her X-rays were normal (as they frequently are with arthritic conditions), but she had an elevated sedimentation rate, which often happens when inflammation or infection is present. I tested for gout and rheumatoid arthritis, but both tests proved negative. Margaret's knee was extremely sore, so I sent her home on crutches and gave her anti-inflammatory medication. The diagnosis: monoarticular arthritis (inflammation of a single joint) of unknown cause.

As far as the trip was concerned, she was in a bind. The last time she was on an airplane was a disaster. Halfway across the ocean she'd had a panic attack and felt she would suffocate. As a result, she hadn't flown since. Fears about traveling in Russia just added to her anxiety.

Margaret's husband insisted he wouldn't go without her. And he was such an overbearing person, she felt he wouldn't be sympathetic to her problem.

I saw her twice a week for the next three weeks and helped her explore her options. What about staying home and letting him take one of his buddies? How about taking tranquilizers? How terrifying was it when she panicked before? What about staying in Stockholm so she wouldn't have to face traveling to Russia? Nothing seemed very satisfactory, but after three weeks of exploring the problem she felt she could tolerate the idea of going on the flight. And by then her knee was nearly well.

Although I don't know why we sometimes experience only subjective symptoms like pain, and at other times physical ones, like swelling and redness, I do know it is important to take notice and discover the cause – physical or emotional.

# CANKER SORES

*You've Got To Get Me Better Doc, Because... Syndrome* may also cause symptoms prior to dreaded medical or dental procedures and other stress-producing events.

Brenda came in because of a large canker sore in her mouth. The medical term for it is aphthous ulcer, which means simply an ulceration or erosion of unknown cause affecting the mucous membranes lining the mouth. Despite many attempts to identify some causative bacteria or virus, medical science has been unable to find any.

I treated her sore with an ointment to relieve the pain and inflammation.

Usually, canker sores run their course in one to two weeks. Brenda's sore had already taken twice that long and wasn't healed. Whenever something takes longer than it should, I'm alert for a hidden issue. She talked about some unhappiness with her job, but it seemed mild, and she seemed fully aware of her feelings. I was definitely puzzled.

Three weeks later, Brenda came back. She had some good news and some bad news. The good news was that the canker sore had finally healed. The bad news was that she had two new, even larger ones.

As I examined them, she said, *I don't know what I'm going to do if these don't clear up, because my dentist won't operate on my jaw as long as I have these in my mouth.* Bingo! It seemed her dentist was going to break her jaw, then wire it shut while it healed. This procedure was supposed to cure her headaches.

*That sounds pretty scary to me,* I said.

She replied, *I hadn't thought about it.*

*If it were me, I'd be concerned,* I said. *I would ask if any nerves could be cut. Could there be complications? What about the risk of being anesthetized? How long would my mouth be wired closed? How would I eat? Would it hurt? Could the operation be a failure?*

I explained that I felt the vast majority of chronic headaches were related to our emotions rather than our teeth. I advised her to get a second opinion from another good oral surgeon. I told her she did not have to have any operation she didn't want to have.

Brenda left with a thoughtful expression on her face. The next time I saw her, she told me she'd decided not to have the operation and the canker sores went away. In addition, her headaches disappeared after she quit the job she had talked to me about.

There are many other examples of *You've Got To Get Me Better Doc, Because... Syndrome* that I could describe to you, but they all have the same trigger mechanism; dreading some upcoming event causes them all, whether it be a trip, a medical procedure, a big meeting, a speech, or something else. Next time you are looking forward to something, and suddenly get symptoms that will keep you from doing it, stop and ask yourself if you've been completely honest with yourself about your feelings.

# 11 DEADLINE & WORKING MOTHER'S SYNDROME

Not uncommonly, we often find ourselves facing some sort of deadline. When the deadlines are unreasonable, we can get sick.

Paula made an emergency appointment to see me before Christmas because she had been throwing up for a week. She knew it wasn't the flu, because she didn't have a fever, chills, or body aches. However, just the thought of food nauseated her.

She was convinced that her problem was nerves and she started talking about quitting her job. She told me she had become executive director of a non-profit organization a few months before, and though she loved the job, the board of directors was driving her crazy. I listened attentively, but was not convinced that that was her problem. When we're aware of what is bothering us, we rarely experience physical symptoms. It's the things that we're *unaware* of that usually cause problems. Also, she had not missed work because of the problem. If the symptom had to do with her job, she should be saying, *You've got to get me better, doc... so I can get back to work.*

While she was talking, she dropped an innocent little comment, *Boy, I've lost eight pounds the hard way in the last week.*

*The hard way? Have you been trying to lose weight?*

*Yes,* she replied. *I started dieting about two weeks ago.*

*Tell me about it.*

*Right after Thanksgiving I decided I wanted to lose weight, so I could fit into my party dress for the holidays.*

*What was your goal?* I asked.

*To lose 20 pounds by Christmas.*

My eyebrows went up. *Twenty pounds is a lot of weight to lose in four weeks. Three months would be more like it. How have you been doing?*

*Well, I lost five pounds the first week and felt pretty good, but the second week I gained a pound.*

*And when did the vomiting start?*

*At the end of the second week.*

I paused. *You know, I think you've got a good friend there in your unconscious mind. That's a pretty effective weight loss technique it's come up with – making you so nauseated that you throw up everything you put in your mouth. I bet it knows that's the only way you could ever lose 20 pounds in a month unless you stopped eating completely. No wonder you said you lost eight pounds the hard way!*

She looked amazed. *You mean this isn't from the stress at work?*

I shook my head. *I don't think so. You're a very determined woman. Are you aware that a sensible weight loss program is five pounds a month?*

*Five pounds a month? You've got to be kidding. That'll take forever!*

Paula took some convincing, but we finally set a goal of February 15th (8 weeks away) to lose her remaining seven or eight pounds. Then I asked her to close her eyes and tell me what she was going to eat the following day. She still could not entertain the idea of eating anything without gagging, so I said in an authoritarian voice, after she had picked out what she wanted for breakfast, *Now eat it all.*

With her eyes closed she began meekly imagining eating. She ate breakfast, lunch and dinner of her choosing in that fashion. Then she opened her eyes and said, *I'm okay now.* That turned it around.

Impossible self-imposed deadlines can cause other problems. When we become impatient to accomplish something, we will sometimes impose insane work schedules on ourselves, driven by our desire to get it over with. In the attempt, we simply exhaust our intellectual, emotional and physical reserves until our unconscious steps in and puts a stop to our self-destructive behavior.

## WORKING MOTHER'S SYNDROME

*Working Mother's Syndrome* is a close cousin to *Deadline Syndrome.*

Along with equal rights for women have come high housing costs, high living costs, high divorce rates, and the necessity for many mothers of young children to enter the work force full time.

The average working mother gets up at 5:00 or 6:00 in the morning, jumps into the shower and gets ready for work. She gets the kids up, cooks breakfast for everyone, makes sure the homework is done, packs the lunches, gets her husband and kids out the door, rushes off to work, works all morning, makes calls checking on child care, compiles a grocery list, works all afternoon, then picks up the groceries and kids. She makes dinner, washes dishes because no one else will, supervises the homework, strong-arms the kids into bed, does a quick load of laundry, pays some bills and then falls exhausted into bed. And then, just as she's dropping off into much-needed sleep, her husband crawls into bed and wants to make love.

The next day is a repeat. When the weekend finally comes, she spends her time cleaning house, running errands, ferrying the kids around, and catching up on all the chores she didn't have time to do during the week.

Sound familiar?

There are some workaholic types who thrive on that schedule, although they, too, will now and then come down with a severe case of the flu. But for the majority, the pace is too hectic.

Non-workaholics need a certain amount of time to rest, relax, indulge in leisure pursuits, and just have fun. It's easy to see how anyone on the schedule outlined above could build up a powerful need for rest.

If you were this young woman's unconscious mind, how would you go about getting her some time off? Right – make her sick. And what kind of physical symptom would put a stop to all the frantic activity? A little back pain won't do it – she'd work right through that. A headache probably wouldn't work either. How about severe weakness? Flu symptoms? Or terrible dizziness and vertigo? These are the kinds of symptoms that tend to appear in people with *Working Mother's Syndrome*. They cause generalized weakness so severe that you literally cannot function out of bed for more than a few minutes. Knees buckle under you. Arms become so weak that you drop things. You often have the symptoms that come with a bad case of the flu.

In its mildest form, it translates into feeling tired, with low energy — *I've been dragging around like a zombie for the past month.* As it becomes more severe, people begin experiencing frightening symptoms involving loss of function in their arms and legs.

One Hispanic woman told me, *Doctor, my hands are so weak I can't make tortillas any more. They feel spastic and I can't move them fast like I used to.* Imagine how you'd feel if your arms, legs, or hands suddenly stopped working. The first thing people suspect is a stroke. If they know someone with multiple sclerosis, they might become worried about that. Often, the diagnosis is chronic fatigue.

As the doctor, I have the authority and the responsibility to prescribe rest for patients with those kinds of symptoms. *I'm going to give you a note for two or three days off work, and I want you to get some help with childcare for the next few days. Take a couple of hot baths a day and get a lot of rest. Doctor's orders!* Unfortunately, I usually have to prescribe this before my patient can allow himself or herself to rest at home with a clear conscience.

Becoming aware that there is a connection between your demanding schedule and your symptoms is very therapeutic. Once you're aware, you can pace and nurture yourself. This might mean a four-hour block of time on a weeknight or weekend to do something you enjoy. An alternative is to exercise thirty minutes a day, read, practice yoga or tai chi, meditate, or listen to a stress-reduction tape. Try closing your eyes periodically during the day — take three deep breaths and feel your body relax.

Many of us are tough and resilient enough to handle a demanding schedule if we aren't wrestling with our own inner conflicts: *Should I stay in this job or would I be happier doing something else? Should I keep seeing this person, even though he or she is not the right one for me? Should I take time for myself, or do I need that time to be with my family? Should I go to work (since we really need the money) or stay home with my baby?* A couple of sessions with a counselor can often help us cope with these problems.

Can ignoring the stress and getting overwhelmed by the demands of life lead to more serious illness? I believe it can.

Is it possible that we haven't found the cause of chronic fatigue and multiple sclerosis because the cause lies in the relationship between our unmet emotional needs and our physical bodies?

Possibilities exist that these are extreme cases of *Deadline and Working Mother's Syndrome,* or one of the other syndromes. There is, however, little interest or funding available for that type of research. Most individuals with multiple sclerosis and other chronic illnesses resist becoming involved in deep psychotherapy and seek physical treatments only. My belief is that the more resistant an individual is to psychotherapy, the more likely there is highly charged material in the unconscious. Even when those patients cooperate, the best therapists and techniques are sometimes unable to uncover their hidden issues.

# 12 RELATIVELY SPEAKING

I n an earlier chapter we looked at how conflicting feelings over a trip to see the in-laws resulted in foot pains. Let's turn our attention to other binds we often find ourselves in with relatives.

## YOU'RE GIVING ME A HEADACHE

Francine, 48, consulted me because she had been suffering from terrible headaches for the past eighteen months. A neurologist had informed her that her headaches were psychosomatic, with no physical cause.

*Francine*, I said, *what was going on in your life about the time these headaches started? Was there anything that involved unhappiness or transition?*

*I did change jobs about that time, but I love my new job! I'm finally doing something I've always wanted to do.*

*What's that?*

*For the past 15 years I worked with learning-disabled children. After the headaches started, I decided it must have been getting to me. I left and went into graphic arts. Unfortunately, changing jobs didn't help. In fact, the headaches are so severe that they're ruining my enjoyment of everything.*

*I see. How about people problems at work?*

*No, everything is great.*

*Okay then, is everything all right between you and your husband?*

Francine replied, *We have a wonderful relationship.*

I decided it was time for the perfect life intervention. I reached out and vigorously shook her hand. *I'd like to congratulate you,* I said. *You're the first person I've ever met who has a perfect life, completely free of any of the problems that the rest of us have.* I kept shaking her hand.

With that, she stammered and said, *Well, doctor... I do have one problem.*

*What's that?*

*My mother is living with us. She moved in 18 months ago.*

*Wasn't that about the time your headaches started?*

As we continued talking, the fact came out that Francine and her husband, who didn't have children, were accustomed to a quiet existence. Their lifestyle abruptly changed when Francine's mother moved in.

Her mother was manic-depressive. Her outrageous behavior was driving Francine crazy and causing tension with her husband. But at the same time, she felt like she couldn't scream at her mentally ill mother. She couldn't ask her to leave as there was no one else to take care of her.

Because of her conflicting feelings, she had been avoiding the situation. Once she connected with the problem, the thought of her mother's disruptive behavior made her furious, sad and hopeless. I advised Francine to work with a counselor on the following issues:

⌒ What her mother did that Francine found irritating.

⌒ Why she felt she couldn't ask her mother to leave.

⌒ What kind of guilt feelings came up at the idea of institutionalizing her mother.

⌒ Her own needs to be a caretaker, be it for her mother or for learning-disabled children.

⌒ How she could enforce periods of peace and quiet around the house.

⌒ What criteria she should use to determine when her mother

would become too ill to live with them.

☞ How much it would cost to move her mother out.

☞ How her mother's presence was affecting her relationship with her husband.

Francine had quit her long-standing job because she assumed it was causing her headaches. In the previous chapter we talked about a woman who thought her job was making her throw up, when her problem really had to do with trying to lose weight too quickly. These examples point out the difficulty of trying to identify your own mind-body interactions. More often than not, your defense mechanisms make you blind to the true source of your problem. In Francine's case, her error had a happy ending. Her mother moved out and Francine ended up in a job she loved.

## You're Getting Under My Skin

Hives, those intensely itchy, irritating welts that can break out all over our bodies in just a few minutes' time, are a common problem.

Elvira came to my office with severe hives. She had no history of taking medication or eating foods that commonly cause hives.

*Elvira*, I said, *often we get hives when we are facing something irritating in our lives. Are you going through a problem?*

*No doctor, everything's fine.*

*No problems at work?*

*No, I like my job.*

*Any tension at home?*

*I've been arguing with my husband some, but no more than usual*, she said with a laugh.

*Arguments usually tend to relieve hives, not cause them, I told her. It's the things we hold inside that cause problems. You don't have any relatives over-staying their welcome do you?*

No.

*Any trips coming up in the next week or so?* I persisted.

*My husband Tom and I are taking his daughter to Disneyland next weekend...*

*Any tension between you and this girl?*

*As a matter of fact, doctor, I'm so furious at the little stinker, I'd like to cancel the trip. We originally planned it for two weekends ago, but we had to cancel it because my back went out!*

Elvira went on to tell me how her 15-year-old stepdaughter lived with her mother. According to Elvira, the girl, Ann, was totally self-centered. The only way Tom could get her to spend a weekend with them was to bribe her. This time it was a trip to Disneyland. Elvira was particularly angry because a month ago she had gone out of her way to show the child she cared about her by buying her an expensive gold necklace for Christmas. Ann sent the necklace back without a thank you. The thought of treating the *ungrateful little stinker* to a weekend in Disneyland was infuriating to Elvira.

Obviously, this is a case of a teenage girl who has been wounded by her parents' divorce, has chosen to live with her mother, and resents her father and his new wife – common enough. Elvira could not stand to watch her husband crawl to the angry teenager, but felt it would be better to keep reaching out with invitations and not bribes. Unfortunately, Tom needed his daughter's company too much to listen to his wife's advice.

Fortunately, Elvira's hives quickly cleared up after our interview. Freely expressing all her pent-up anger and frustration, and making her husband aware of his daughter's emotional blackmail solved her problem.

---

Ellen came to see me after experiencing a week of intensely itchy, red, hot swellings on her face, behind her ears, and over her chest and forearms. Her condition is called angioedema, which is related to but somewhat different than hives. Ellen had two daughters, ages 20 and 24. Despite her high hopes for college and good careers for her daughters, they both became pregnant right out of high school. The older daughter was living with her husband. The younger daughter, who was still at home with Ellen, received public assistance, acted irresponsibly, wouldn't help keep the house clean, and constantly dumped her child on Ellen.

When I asked why she didn't tell her to leave, Ellen asked, *How could I kick my daughter and granddaughter out?* Her daughter was clearly taking advantage of Ellen's soft-heartedness. I asked Ellen what she thought *Dear Abby* would tell her to do. Armed with Abby's and my support, she laid down the law. Her angioedema problem cleared right up.

## BURIED ALIVE!

Do you ever feel like you're forgetting to breathe? Yet when you fill your lungs up, it is strangely unsatisfying, like you can't quite get a deep enough breath? If so, you may be hyperventilating, the first step on the way to a panic attack.

A full-blown panic attack is obvious, but like many conditions panic disorder varies in severity from very mild to very severe. When it is mild, the symptoms are vague and the diagnosis is easy to miss. This is important because hyperventilation and panic are very common, and when not treated early and effectively tend to progress to extremely disturbing, often disabling symptoms.

The first symptom of mild hyperventilation is often the sighing I mentioned above. A family member may notice and say something. Just as often the first symptom is a feeling of lightheadedness or dizziness. People say they just don't feel right. They feel *"weird"* or *"spaced-out"*. These symptoms tend to come up during periods of inactivity, typically when you are driving, sitting around, standing in line at the market, or lying down to go to bed at night. They may waken you from sleep in the middle of the night.

The next symptom is usually funny feelings around your body. Numbness or tingling of the fingertips or around the mouth is common. A hot, flushed feeling in the face, a lump in the throat, and a rising feeling of anxiety often follow this. These symptoms may progress to a full-blown panic attack with chest pains that mimic a heart attack, pains down the arms, a feeling of suffocation, palpitations where you feel your heart is going to pound out of your chest, and a terrifying feeling that you are going to die. Usually the fear is of a heart attack or a stroke.

The first thing you have to know if you have had symptoms like these is that hyperventilation and panic can't harm you. It's a terrifying experience, but it is not dangerous. It can't hurt your heart, and it won't cause a stroke. Like any medical problem, the cure lies in understanding the problem and directing your attention to the underlying cause. Here's how I explain it to my patients.

Imagine that you laid down in the afternoon for a nice relaxing nap and dozed off. Then someone came in and made a terrible mistake. They thought you were dead and put you in a coffin 6 feet underground. Imagine what you would feel like waking up in that coffin. You would panic. *"I'm trapped! I'm going to die!"* You would start to gasp for air. Your throat would feel like it was closing off. Your heart would race. And you would be in a state of absolute terror. Your rapid breathing would throw off the acid-base balance of your blood, making you feel worse. This causes the numbness, tingling, flushing, weird feelings, and muscle cramps that are part of the picture.

This, of course, is a claustrophobic reaction. It's a completely understandable and appropriate response under the circumstances. Hyperventilation and panic attacks are a form of claustrophobia, but they are not caused by being physically confined. They occur when we have been caught in some situation that has been smoldering along in our lives that has been making us feel trapped. We don't know how to resolve this problem, so without even realizing it we push it into the back of our mind. We avoid thinking about it and do our best to go on with our life. We get busy. When we are busy, it helps keep that trapped feeling from coming up into our awareness. But, when the action stops, the mind has a harder time containing that feeling, and the body's physical reactions start to arise. We need air, we feel lightheaded and anxious, and so on.

The tricky part is that the situation that is causing the problem does not come into awareness, only the physical symptoms connected to it. People have a hard time accepting that such violent, real, physical symptoms could be caused by stress. "Doctor, this can't be from stress. I'm not under any stress today. In fact, everything in my life is fine right now, better than it's been in a long time. Today was an absolutely normal day and I was just driving my car when this hit me. There has to be something wrong."

Once a patient understands that it is not today's stress that is making them hyperventilate, but something difficult that has been building up in them and needs talking about, they will usually recover promptly and completely.

There will always be resistance to talking about the situation that is at the root of the problem. After all, the reason it was suppressed in the first place was that it was upsetting, and we didn't know how to solve it. The doctor needs to ask the right questions in the right way. Often the patient starts talking about issues that have nothing to do with the panic attack. The real problem is usually a bit buried, and it takes some probing, time, and trust to come out. We all face difficulties in this life, and the important thing is to begin talking about your problems, even if they seem minor. This will lead you to the source of your hyperventilation and panic attacks.

Panic attacks can arise from any difficult problem in life that we don't know how to solve. Here's an example that has to do with relatives.

Leah came in complaining about attacks of breathlessness, dizziness, chest pressure, weakness, palpitations, and panicky feelings. The spells scared her half to death. After a medical evaluation turned up no signs of heart, lung, or other serious problems, I told her that she had the classic symptoms of hyperventilation and panic attacks. I explained that the problem is like an emotional claustrophobic reaction —it comes about when we subconsciously feel trapped by some situation in our lives. Our body reacts the same way it would if we woke up trapped six feet underground in a coffin, namely, by panicking, fighting for breath, and being terrified that we are going to die. Leah assured me that *everything was fine,* but after some further probing, I turned up her story.

Just before the symptoms started, her twin sister had phoned from Missouri to say she was getting married and Leah had to come to her wedding. She really wanted to – or at least a big part of her wanted to go. However, there was another part of her that didn't want to go to her sister's wedding – a part that was only partly conscious.

*I've talked to my husband, and we don't have the money right now to take two weeks off to drive to St. Louis for this wedding. I don't know what I'm going to do.*

Leah was fully conscious of that part. If money was the real problem, I doubt she would have been hyperventilating.

But then there was the unconscious part.

*My mother has been pressuring me to come back. She and my*

*whole family live there. Mother was quite upset when I moved to California two years ago with my fiancé. She always makes me feel guilty.*

Her mother, who was in her early forties, had quit working three years before due to a heart problem. When Leah turned 18, she took over all the homemaking responsibilities. Mom was sick and somebody had to take responsibility.

Mom stayed sick. Leah felt like an indentured servant who was expected to spend the rest of her life taking care of her parents. But she didn't complain, especially to her mother. Leah felt tremendously relieved, however, when she met her future husband and they moved 2,000 miles away to California.

The problem was that Leah, despite the 2,000 miles between them, found it difficult to stand up to her mother. Once before, she had felt compelled to go home at her mother's urging and against her own will. When she arrived, her family acted like they expected her to do all the housework. And she did it. Leah summed up the situation by saying to me, *When I go back there, it's like I'm their maid.*

Worse, her mother wouldn't come to California for Leah's wedding. Her sister, also, was unable to make it.

*Why do I have to jump when they call?* Leah asked.

She blanched when I suggested she tell her mother how she felt. Her body language indicated that she was simply not emotionally prepared to do that. I encouraged her to stay home, if she and her husband really couldn't afford the trip. I pointed out that it was a wonderful opportunity to say no to her mother. I told her that she needed to stand up for what she felt was best for her. And I suggested that if she decided not to go, she send her sister flowers, with a note expressing her regrets that she was unable to be there and wishing the couple happiness.

Leah felt like a big weight had been lifted off her shoulders. She was amazed, because she'd told me things she had never told anybody. She really did want to go to her sister's wedding. At the same time, however, she didn't want to go, because of the *maid issue,* money concerns, smoldering hurt feelings over her mother not coming to her wedding, and a reluctance to be lured back to where her mother could manipulate her.

Her case points out how we can work ourselves into a corner by not being able to say *no*. Leah needed to say *no*. People who have been raised by domineering parents all too frequently emerge from childhood completely incapable of speaking up to authority figures. The inability to stand up for ourselves gets us into situations like this. Feeling trapped frequently leads to hyperventilation and panic attacks, with their disturbing array of physical symptoms.

## ROAST NOSE

Flora, a 30-year-old woman, came to my office because of a large, red, bulbous swelling on the tip of her nose. She looked like Rudolph the Red-Nosed Reindeer. I examined her nose and told her we would try to get it to go away with hot soaks and powerful antibiotics. When she was about to leave, Flora asked me, *Doctor, how long is this going to take? I have to be at my parents' silver wedding anniversary celebration in about ten days...* Sound familiar? *You've gotta get me better doc, because...*

*You should be better by then,* I replied. *Boils usually run their course in about a week.* I was busy, so I didn't interview her at that time but waited to see what would happen.

She returned for a recheck three days later. Her nose was bigger, redder and more bulbous than ever, but the abscess was still not ready to lance. I gave her more antibiotics, told her to continue to soak her nose, and to return in two days. When she came back, her nose was ridiculous looking, but at least it was finally ready to lance. After lancing it I asked, *Flora, how do you feel about going to the anniversary celebration with your nose looking this way?*

*Not good,* she said with a little smile. *I'm supposed to get up and give a speech.*

Since I wanted her to get in touch with her suppressed fears about being in front of people, I said, *That's hard even with a normal nose. When I first started speaking in front of people, I'd get so panicked, I could hardly talk.*

She went on, *Yes, it's hard for me. I'm supposed to 'roast' them. I've never done that before, and I can't think of anything to 'roast' them about.*

Some people are natural 'roasters.' They are relaxed in front of people and can get into that kind of humor. Flora was too nervous to do it naturally.

Just before she left, I asked Flora what she would do about the anniversary if her nose still looked the same by the weekend.

She answered without hesitation, *I'll skip it.*

Two days later she returned for a final recheck. Her nose was nearly back to normal. When I asked her about the weekend, now only three days away, she said in a resigned tone of voice, *I guess I'm going to have to go.* Without her boil, she had no excuse.

If I hadn't intervened and lanced the boil, I'm sure she would have missed the anniversary party. However, I'd like to believe that my conversation with Flora about her stage fright did almost as much for her quick recovery as did my scalpel.

# 13 How We Work Ourselves Sick

*aw Deal Syndrome* is the most common hidden issue in work-related injuries. There are sixteen additional syndromes I see frequently in my practice that concern people who work themselves sick. Each of them reflects a different inner need that our unconscious fills with a symptom.

## 1. On the Road Again
### (the need to be home)

Sam came to see me because of a sore left elbow. During the previous two days, it had become warm, reddened and swollen. When I examined it, I found that the bony promontory at the tip of the elbow was completely covered by a large sack of fluid. That bone is called the olecranon, and when the slippery membrane that covers it just beneath the skin becomes inflamed, the condition is called olecranon bursitis.

I explained to Sam that striking something with the point of the elbow, or leaning on a hard surface with the elbows for a long period of time usually causes it. He couldn't recall doing any of that, so I began to wonder if he had a hidden issue.

I asked, *When does it bother you the most, Sam?*

*It bothers me most when I drive my car. I'm getting ready to go out of state. I'll be doing a lot of driving and I'm wondering if I should go now that the elbow has flared up.*

*Oh? What's the occasion for the trip?*

*My business requires that I spend December through March every year out of state. I was just getting ready to leave when this thing flared up.*

*Every year for four months... You have a wife and two children. How do you feel about being away from them for so long?*

*I hate it, he said. It didn't seem to bother me so much when my kids were little, but now that they're teenagers, I really want to be home with them.*

*What about a transfer to another position in your company?*

He shook his head. *I'm in agribusiness. The whole operation here shuts down in December every year.*

What about another job?

*Agribusiness is all I know. I have a good job, a lot of benefits. And I'm looking at college expenses for my two kids in the next few years. If I switched companies, I would lose seniority.*

I nodded and gently broached the idea that the situation could be causing him so much stress that it would contribute to his elbow problem. He found this hard to believe, so I dropped it. I left him with the idea that I felt it was very important for him to resolve the problem in some way.

I took X-rays of his elbow. They were negative. There were no signs of arthritis or calcium deposits. I drew some blood and tested him for gout. That was negative. I put the arm in a sling and gave him some anti-inflammatory pills, telling him to be careful to protect the elbow, apply heat, and see me in five days.

Five days later, Sam returned. The fluid accumulation was even larger than before. Since he needed to get on the road, I drew the fluid out with a needle and put in some long-acting cortisone.

He returned three days later with a worried look on his face. *My left elbow is better, doctor, but now my right one has swelled up!* He rolled up his sleeve and sure enough, his right elbow was warm, red, and swollen. At that point, I referred him to an arthritis specialist.

I didn't see Sam again until he came into my office about a year later with one of his children. He looked well. I asked, *Sam, whatever happened to those elbows?*

*They bothered me for months until I quit my job and opened my own business, he said. My elbows haven't bothered me a bit since then. I think you were probably right about my previous job causing the problem, doctor.*

Sam's swollen elbows were his unconscious mind's attempt to tell him that he was at a crisis point. Something had to change. When the message was suppressed in the left elbow with medication, it transferred to the right elbow. When he listened and acted on the problem, he recovered.

Like Sam, most of us have a basic need to spend a certain amount of time at home. When that need is not met, our unconscious may make us too sick to travel.

## BE IT EVER SO HUMBLE...

Louise stopped by my office with her husband to get her arthritis prescription refilled. Her husband was a long-haul truck driver and they were in the middle of another cross-country marathon together. Shortly after they were married, four years earlier, she'd found that she couldn't handle his long absences. Also, she was sure he was sleeping with other women when he was on the road. She solved the problem by becoming his bunkmate. For the past three years, they had been riding around the United States in the cab of his semi-truck and trailer. They slept in the bunk behind the cab and showered with the rest of the guys at the truck stops.

I asked her where their home was.

*Texas,* she replied. *We bought an acre near a lake and put a double-wide on it.*

*How often do you get back there?*

*About once every month or six weeks. We stay about two or three days, then hit the road again.* She paused. *Sometimes it brings tears to my eyes just closin' the screen door.*

I put my hand on her shoulder and she began to cry quietly. Louise was in a terrible bind. She had to choose between jealousy and aching loneliness on the one hand, and a totally unsatisfying, nomadic existence in a man's world on the other. Roughly a year after going on the road with her husband, she began developing arthritis in her shoulders and hands.

I told both of them that it was very important for her health that she spend more time at home. They seemed to make the connection and understand the importance of that. They drove away in their truck and I never heard from them again.

# ...There's No Place Like Home

While I was taking her medical history for another problem, Evelyn told me that she had to stop traveling because she had become allergic to the sheets in the hotels.

*Allergic to hotel sheets?*

*Yes. I don't know if it's the commercial detergents they use, but I had to stop traveling because it got to the point that every time I went to bed in a hotel room, I would start itching and break out with a terrible rash.*

Were you traveling on business or pleasure?

*I used to go all over the world on extended buying trips. I hated to quit because I made such great money.*

Do you react to your own sheets at home?

*You know, it's funny, but I never have.*

That is an example of how strategic our unconscious is when it chooses symptoms for us. Evelyn's unconscious knew she couldn't bear to walk away from her terrific income and prestigious job. But it also knew she was burned out from all that traveling. An allergy to hotel sheets was a very creative move on the part of her subconscious. What a perfect metaphor. *My skin gets unbearably irritated sleeping in hotel beds. I can't stand it anymore.* That substitutes nicely for her inability to say, *I can't stand living out of a suitcase for one more day. I need to be home.*

## 2. Home Stretch Syndrome
### (the need to escape a job where we are burned out)

Some people are lucky enough to find work that remains varied, interesting, and stimulating, as they grow older. Others find themselves locked into jobs where they've lost interest. Many such jobs are hard to give up because of the money or the fear that another job isn't available. Still others don't actively dislike their jobs; they just find themselves tired and worn down after years of hard work. When that happens, it's human nature to look forward to retirement.

We don't know it, but when we get to the point where we're counting the days until we retire, we are vulnerable to an accident or injury that will disable us. Frequently, injury is the only way we can effectively retire a year or two early and not sacrifice monetary benefits.

We are particularly susceptible to *Home Stretch Syndrome* if we have a safety net in the form of worker's compensation benefits, disability insurance, mortgage, car payment, and health insurance that take effect when we become disabled.

It seems crazy that someone would choose injury and pain to get out of a job. But I have seen many cases where, if a person is burned out at work and the unconscious mind knows he or she can escape through an injury with minimal economic loss, it may conclude that a year or two of physical pain is worth it. If, on the other hand, our unconscious mind knows that we and our loved ones are going to go hungry if we become disabled, it will get us better because the need to survive replaces our need to escape boredom and a job we no longer want to do. That is food for thought when we consider buying a disability insurance policy. I personally carry no disability insurance. I want my unconscious mind to know that I can't afford to be disabled.

## SMALL BUSINESSPERSON'S SYNDROME

What happens when there are penalties attached to becoming disabled? Small business owners rarely get sick or disabled. If you ask them why, they usually laugh and say, *I can't afford to get sick!* They are not covered by worker's compensation insurance because they are owners, not workers. There is no one to take over for them if they become seriously ill. If they are off work for more than a day or two, their whole business begins to fall apart, and with it their source of livelihood. Those are heavy penalties.

## 3. POWER STRUGGLE
### (THE NEED TO WIN OR BE RIGHT)

We get into disagreements with our boyfriends, girlfriends, husbands, wives, children, parents, coworkers, creditors, bosses, and employees on a regular basis. Sometimes the disagreements turn into power struggles where both parties are determined to win, no matter what the cost.

Christine, a woman of about 40, came into my office because of a severe pain in her right shoulder that prevented her from working. When I asked how it happened, she said with a sarcastic tone, *I guess I'm being punished.*

*Oh?*

*I'm a school bus driver. I'm also the union steward for our local. Our regional administrator is a real jerk. We got into an argument yesterday, and he decided to punish me by making me drive an older bus with a mechanical door opener. My regular bus has a button you push that opens the door. The older bus has a long arm that goes over the door. Pulling on it must have strained my shoulder, because it started acting up right after he put me in that bus. I had to leave work and come here.*

X-rays and examination of Christine's shoulder revealed no abnormality other than her pain, but I couldn't return her to work, because her arm hurt so much. I put it in a sling. In spite of my treatment, her shoulder wouldn't get better. I finally referred her to a specialist, who also found only *strained muscles*. He had no choice but to keep her off work until they gave her a bus that didn't require any heavy pushing or pulling with her right arm. Her need to win her power struggle with her boss was stronger than her desire to be well.

I want to emphasize that Christine's pains were real, and consciously she wanted to get better. The side effect of her *victory* was that her shoulder ached constantly and interfered with her sleep. It's a hollow victory when, by *winning*, we sacrifice our health and our ability to be gainfully employed. Power struggles often occur between husbands and wives, and there, too, our unconscious may choose to give us bodily symptoms. Earlier I related a story about a woman who got a terrible rash on her hand that prevented her from doing her husband's bookkeeping. It was a clear example of a symptom brought on by a domestic power struggle. If you are angry about the way your husband treats you, but find him too frightening to confront directly, you may develop headaches, bladder infections, or painful vaginal conditions that deny him sex. Sometimes a man will deny a woman sex as a way of getting back at her, but that occurs less often. He may become impotent, simply lose interest, or develop a variety of physical complaints.

In male-female relationships, women suffer from those kinds of symptoms more often than men, because traditionally, in most societies, men have been dominant. It's the women who need to call on their bodies for extra help. At work, however, the male-female issues are not as important, although they do still occur. There, it's the employees, male or female, who need help from their bodies to win battles against their powerful superiors.

## 4. Look What You Did to Me
### (power struggles between coworkers)

Power struggles also occur between coworkers. Theresa had gone to work in the kitchen of a Mexican restaurant. She was the only female on the kitchen crew, and for some reason the guys who worked there took a dislike to her. They refused to take the ten-pound box of grated cheese off the shelf for her. Since she was short, she had to stand on a stool to reach it. The guys were tall and the box was easily within their reach. When she asked, they said, *Get it yourself. That's part of the job. If you can't hack it, leave.*

Naturally, Theresa told herself she wasn't going to let it bother her. Can you guess what happened? As she stood on the stool reaching for the cheese box, the box fell and struck her shoulder a glancing blow. She came into my office in tears, complaining of terrible pain. There were no marks on her shoulder, and her X-rays were normal. I put her arm in a sling, gave her some pain medication, and sent her back to work with a note saying she had to wear the sling for a day or two.

Theresa returned to work wearing her sling like a badge. It said better than any words could say to those men in the kitchen, *"Look what you did to me"*. When the boss told them to start getting the box of cheese down for her, her shoulder promptly improved.

## 5. I Hate This
### (the need to avoid physical discomfort)

There are lots of reasons why we wish to avoid certain jobs. The job might be too smelly, too messy, too dirty, too hot, too cold, too dangerous, too hard, too fast, too slow, or too noisy. Sooner or later, most of us get stuck doing some job we hate. We can't refuse to do it. We don't want to call in sick. We could tell our boss we really don't want to do it, but it's very likely he'd say, *Do it anyway.* We could quit and avoid it that way, but most of us can't or won't do that. What does that leave? I don't need to tell you there is one sure-fire way to get out of a job like this – get sick or injured.

José came in complaining of low-back pain. A lettuce cutter, he said his back hurt too much to continue working. He said it had bothered him in the same way the summer before. He claimed he'd never twisted it or fallen down. It just started aching so much he couldn't continue working. He sincerely believed he had been injured, and I believed he was in pain. José's X-rays and examination were normal, except for back stiffness and pain when he bent over. I had no choice but to send him home from work.

On his next visit I interviewed him, wondering what hidden issue he might have. He seemed to be well enough adjusted. As I questioned him, he volunteered that he hated working in the heat. He said he felt comfortable as long as it was cold or cool outside, but in the summer he was miserable. The hot sun just seemed to drain his strength.

José's unconscious mind had learned exactly how to get him out of that terribly uncomfortable job.

———⇒◦⇐———

Don worked in a cardboard box manufacturing plant. He disliked working in the room where they ran the boxes through the hot wax machine to waterproof them. He found both the heat and the smell objectionable. Also, since it was not his regular job, he resented being made to work there.

Every time Don was sent into the *wet room*, as they called it, his back would start to hurt so much they had to send him to the doctor, who would invariably send him home to rest for a day or two. Finally, it became so obvious to everybody that being sent to the wet room brought on the back pains, the plant manager confronted him and made it clear that was unacceptable. From then on, Don did his time in the wet room. His back either stopped hurting or he kept quiet about it.

———⇒◦⇐———

Paul was promoted from his old job, which involved being outdoors and having freedom of movement, to a desk job. His new job was an advancement, but he hated being cooped up. He came to me complaining of headaches. *This headache makes me feel like I need to get out and get some air,* he said. That was a clue to his suppressed feelings. I suggested he take a five- or ten-minute break every couple of hours and walk out of the building. He also decided to put posters of mountain scenery on his office walls. After that, his headaches improved dramatically.

------➤-◊-◄------

These cases all involved discomfort with some aspect of the physical environment: too hot, too closed in, too smelly, and so forth. There is another important reason we can hate a particular job, which doesn't involve us being uncomfortable physically.

## 6. I'm a Legend in My Own Mind
### (THE NEED TO AVOID WORK WE FEEL IS BENEATH US)

When we are forced by circumstances to do work that doesn't fit our self-image, we often become sick or injured and unable to work.

Jack, in his late 30s, had worked in general construction for fifteen or twenty years. It was always something different, and he liked building things. For the previous four months, however, his left elbow had bothered him while he was working. When he came to see me, his chief concern was that he might have to give up construction work. X-rays and an examination showed no evidence of arthritis, only a painful elbow.

*What would you do if you gave up construction?* I asked him.

*I like photography,* he replied. *I've sold a few pictures and I've started thinking about going into the business. I need to be more than just a construction worker. I have a lot of friends who are professionals, and frankly, I feel like a clod next to them.*

It wasn't the first time I had heard that from a construction worker. Young men in their twenties generally like the macho, outdoors aspect of the construction trades. Some continue to enjoy their work for years. Many, however, begin to feel the urge to get into white-collar or professional work.

Jack went on, *I never felt this way until about six months ago. I got involved with a woman who is an accountant. I started hanging out with her friends, who are all professionals, bankers, doctors, lawyers... you know. That's when I really started feeling this way.*

His new relationship had suddenly made him feel embarrassed about the kind of work he did. Talking to me didn't make his feelings magically disappear. I saw him weekly for a month or two to give him some support. He decided to quit construction. Over the next four months he gradually built up his photography business. His identity crisis reached such a peak that he even changed his name. His elbow, however, continued to bother him just enough to make him feel he'd better avoid any kind of heavy manual work.

Six months later, Jack came back to see me. The relationship with the lady accountant had run its course. After being away from construction, he realized he actually liked it a lot. As soon as he once again became comfortable with his work, his elbow pain completely disappeared and didn't return.

As Jack's case points out, there are any number of reasons why we feel our work is beneath us. We may feel that our job is somehow unsuitable for the company we are keeping. Another common situation occurs when we are highly trained but haven't been able to find employment in our field. Still another is, when we have worked in management, but are now a lowly worker, taking orders from a supervisor we don't respect. All of those situations are fertile soil for hidden issues that can sideline us with some physical problem.

## 7. PORT-A-POTTY SYNDROME

We human beings are social animals. It is important that our group accept us. We all know how cruel schoolchildren can be when they identify *targets* that react to teasing. They make those kids' lives miserable, until pretty soon the teased children mysteriously become sick. As adults, we never engage in that kind of immature behavior. Or do we?

I worked for years in California's Salinas Valley, an enormously productive agricultural area. Crews of primarily Hispanic farm laborers work the fields. They are transported to and from the fields on special buses owned by the growers. The buses have chemical toilets mounted on little trailers that tag along behind. The workers use the toilets during their breaks and at the end of the day, before getting back on the bus.

Now and then there is a worker who is not terribly popular with the rest of the crew. Invariably, someone has a great idea and the plan goes like clockwork. The unpopular worker goes into the toilet and as soon as his co-workers see him close the door, everybody piles on the bus and they take off. The bus jolts over the ruts at the side of the road and the driver hits the brakes. The worker pulls his pants up and opens the door to see everyone on the bus laughing at him.

If that happened to everybody's favorite on the crew, I would never hear about it. I get the ones who are the targets. They come into my office with pain all over their bodies. I call it *total-body pain syndrome*. I have never seen one person yet with any visible bruising, but of course, it isn't their bodies that are injured, it's their feelings.

Not long ago, I saw a patient whose diagnosis was multiple traumatic injuries. She had been off work since her injury two months before. I thought to myself, this is a case of *Port-a-potty Syndrome*. I reviewed her chart from the beginning and saw her sad story: *Patient was locked in a chemical toilet when the bus began moving.*

These patients have terrible body pains that simply won't go away. As time goes by, their symptoms migrate mysteriously around their bodies and we end up X-raying them until I'm surprised they don't glow in the dark. It's usually two or three months before they are well enough to go back to work.

*Port-a-potty Syndrome* doesn't just happen to farm workers. It can happen to anyone who is humiliated by his or her co-workers. Herman worked on a machine in a factory. His workstation was situated, so that the rest of the crew was to his left. Because of an attendance problem, when the end of the pay period came, Herman was the only one who didn't get a bonus check.

The guys decided it would be great for laughs to have a little fun with Herman. They all got their bonus checks out and waited. Then, right on cue, one of them shouted, *Hey Herman!* When Herman turned to look at them, they all held their bonus checks up at arm's length. Herman turned back to his work and did his best to shrug it off. That same morning they did it twice more. Suddenly the left side of Herman's face, the side exposed to the crew, began to droop and became paralyzed. It appeared he was having a stroke. He was rushed to the emergency room. Fortunately, he hadn't had a stroke. It was an acute episode of Bell's palsy.

Bell's palsy involves sudden and inexplicable swelling around the facial nerve, where it goes through a narrow, bony passageway in the bottom of the skull as it exits the brain. We have two facial nerves, one on each side, and each one carries the nervous impulses that control the muscles on half of our face. When there is sudden swelling around the nerve, it gets knocked out of commission and our face droops on that side, mimicking a stroke.

It's not a stroke, however, and in roughly 90 percent of the cases, patients fully recover in about three months. No one knows what causes it, and there is little effective treatment for it. The nerve regenerates itself with the passage of time. I've seen several cases of Bell's palsy that appeared after a symbolic *slap-in-the-face*.

## 8. I CAN'T FACE THIS
### (THE NEED TO ESCAPE EMOTIONAL DISCOMFORT)

It's possible to find ourselves in all kinds of situations that make us very uncomfortable, and our unconscious has its own symbolic ways of protecting the side of the body that is exposed to the problem. We can accept the fact that if we are exposed to poison oak or poison ivy on one side of our face, that side of our face erupts. What is so novel about the idea that if we are exposed to a toxic emotional influence on one side of our body, we may react with uncomfortable symptoms on that side?

Stephanie was 18 years old and on her first job as a secretary in a small family business. There were only three people there: Stephanie, her boss, and his wife. They all worked in one large office and things were fine when she started work.

After she had been there a short time, however, her employer's wife started taking Stephanie out to lunch and confiding in her about her marital problems. What Stephanie had thought was a happy family business was really just the opposite. Her boss and his wife were going through a bitter divorce. Over the next few weeks, Stephanie became privy to all the gory details about the man she had to sit next to and conduct a business relationship with on a day-to-day basis.

After several weeks, Stephanie awoke one Monday morning with excruciating pain when she attempted to turn her head to the right. She could turn her head to the left and look straight ahead, but she couldn't turn it to the right at all. She came into my office about nine that morning, wanting me to fix her neck so she could return to work.

After hearing her story, I felt certain her symptoms were related to her discomfort at work, but I couldn't fathom why it was manifesting itself as a wry neck, which is what that symptom is called. I gave Stephanie some muscle relaxants, pain medicine, and a soft foam collar for her neck. As I was writing a note excusing her from work for the next few days, I suddenly thought to ask who sat on her right side at work.

Apparently, she had reached the point where she felt uncomfortable knowing all about her employer's secrets and she simply couldn't look him in the eye anymore. Her unconscious was taking care of the problem. It made her so uncomfortable and caused her so much pain that she couldn't turn her head to look at him.

My insight proved correct. Stephanie quit her job that week. She didn't have the skills to confront the wife and say what Ann Landers would have probably told her: *Please Mrs. So-and-So, you're going to have to stop talking to me about your personal affairs. It's making me too uncomfortable. I'm going to start taking lunch hours on my own. I hope you understand. Thank you.*

If Stephanie had possessed the communication skills to do that, she might have retained her position. As it was, she had little choice but to use her incapacitating symptoms as a convenient excuse to escape the situation.

## 9. I DON'T WANNA GO
### (THE FEAR OF HEIGHTS)

This syndrome is about the fear of heights. Typically, the problem occurs when a man has been hired to work as a carpenter and finds himself required to work at heights that are terrifying to him. This often happens during the first week or two on the job. An injury suddenly occurs that sidelines the worker — most often a back strain that forces him to quit.

The other common scenario is when a man has a close call and has the heck scared out of him. This happened to Roland, who worked on an oil rig off the Texas coast. Those rigs are high above the water and Roland had a close call, nearly falling to his death. He was taken back to the mainland to recover and although the injury wasn't serious, the experience was – it caused a symptom you should be familiar with reading about by now. After a week, Roland was shipped back to the oil rig. About three-quarters of the way out, he developed severe pains in his lower back. The boat dropped some supplies and a few people off at the drilling platform, and headed back to shore with Roland. When I heard about his case, he had been disabled for over six months.

Roland was terrified of falling to his death, pure and simple. His unconscious mind was protecting him. In all likelihood he could have returned to a normal, productive existence with proper treatment directed at the underlying cause.

## 10. Too Much Too Soon
### (THE NEED TO AVOID GETTING IN OVER YOUR HEAD)

Most of us desire advancement. We want to better ourselves, which means going for promotions, higher pay, and the perks that go with them. Any change, however, even if we want it, is stressful. With promotion comes added responsibility and power. Some of us thrive on those things and some of us find them a heavy burden. Promotion can also bring discomfort because it affects our interpersonal relationships at work.

Anything that makes us uncomfortable generates a need to escape from the discomfort. When the need to escape builds to a high level, you can probably guess who's standing in the wings ready to help — our good old unconscious mind.

There are three common scenarios that deserve mention here. The first affects young managers who are being moved into supervisory positions that involve more responsibility than they are able to handle.

Tom was a young manager for a restaurant chain. He had recently received a promotion and had been put in charge of the kitchen staff — a crew of 12 people, many of them older than Tom. His promotion involved transferring to a different restaurant in the chain, where he didn't know anyone. Shortly after his promotion, Tom developed a pain in his thumb that wouldn't go away.

When we talked about his situation, it became obvious that while he wanted advancement, he was feeling totally stressed and overwhelmed by the weight of the promotion. As with the others I've discussed with you, he would not admit this to himself.

Finally, after a lot of soul-searching over the next two months, Tom decided to take a demotion and return to his former position at his old restaurant. His thumb pain cleared up almost immediately. Had he gone into counseling and worked through his discomfort with his new responsibilities, he very likely could have kept the promotion.

The second common scenario is when a production worker is promoted to supervise his or her former co-workers. Top management needs to prepare such people for the fact that they may go through an uncomfortable period of adjustment. They need to be forewarned that close friendships may become cool and distant and that jealousies may occur. Former co-workers may resist taking orders from them, and they will need upper management to support them in dealing with this. People who are placed in positions like this, with no support or preparation, often develop disabling symptoms that interfere with work.

The third and most common situation occurs when people who don't want to be put in charge are put in charge. They're not being paid to be in charge, it's not their job to be in charge, and they're scared to be in charge.

Joan, 18, worked in a dress shop. Her boss left town for a few days and put her in charge. Joan had never been in charge of anything in her whole life, much less a business. She came in to see me the morning her boss left, because her shoulders had started hurting so much she couldn't raise her arms enough to get the dresses off the racks.

*What am I going to do?* she asked. *I can't work like this, and my boss is going to kill me if I can't. There is no one else to take care of the store.*

Joan was in so much pain she had to go home. I don't know what happened in the store, but she certainly wasn't there.

———◦———

Gwynne didn't have a case of *too much, too soon,* she had a case *of too much, period.* She had been hired to work as an administrative assistant at a private school. She was a capable woman, and her boss gradually abdicated responsibility to her, putting Gwynne completely in charge of setting up courses and enrolling students. Gwynne resented that more and more as time went on. She felt she had been hired as an assistant, and she felt it was irresponsible of her boss to load all that work and responsibility on her.

There would be nothing wrong with that had they both understood what was expected. The problem was that the boss didn't explain it to Gwynne when she hired her. The situation had just spontaneously evolved.

At that time Gwynne's anus started to hurt. When she came into my office, it had been hurting for three months.

*When does it bother you?* I asked.

*Mainly when I get up in the morning, or when I'm getting ready to go to work. Usually it stops hurting about ten or eleven in the morning.*

Gwynne had no hemorrhoids or anything else to account for her pain. Her treatment consisted of two things. First we discussed exactly what she wanted her job description to be. Second, we role-played talking to her boss about it. That was frightening for her, but after a couple of tries, she got into it. She sat down with her boss the next day and talked to her about her frustrations. Her boss felt terrible. She had no idea it had been bothering Gwynne so much. She liked Gwynne and valued her as an employee. She renegotiated her position and gave her what she wanted. Gwynne's three-month *pain in the rear* disappeared completely within five days and did not recur.

The only medical treatment Gwynne needed was some encouragement from her doctor to have a long-overdue, heart-to-heart talk with her boss.

## 11. I Told Them, I Told Them, But They Just Don't Care
### (THE NEED TO BE HEARD AND CARED FOR)

*I told them, I told them, but they just don't care*, are often the first words out of a patient's mouth when he or she comes into my office to be treated for a work injury.

Have you ever complained about some faulty piece of equipment or hazardous condition at work that you felt posed a danger and had your superiors shrug it off? It's demoralizing to have our bosses react as if they don't care, or as if they think our complaints are trivial. We need to feel that our superiors are concerned about our safety and comfort; it's hurtful and infuriating when they're not.

Susan was sent to my office from work because of an injury she suffered during a fall. She was in tears from the terrible back pain and the first thing she said to me was, *I kept telling them I was going to hurt myself on that potato box. They just don't care.*

*What happened?* I asked

*I work in a restaurant kitchen. They expect me to lift a box of potatoes that must weigh sixty or seventy pounds. I hurt my back once and the doctor told me I should be careful about lifting heavy things. At work, we're supposed to pick up this huge box, carry it over to our workstation, get the potatoes out and then carry it back. I told my supervisor that it was too heavy for me and asked if I could just take out the potatoes I needed and put them in my apron. He said, 'No, you have to carry the box over. That's how we've always done it. Everyone else does it that way, and if I make an exception for you, I'll have to do it for everyone else. Besides, no one else has ever complained about it, and I don't think it's all that heavy.' It's obvious he doesn't care about my back. This morning, as I picked up the box, I turned to go over to my workstation, slipped on the wet floor, and fell. Now my back is killing me, thanks to him.*

X-rays of Susan's back were normal. She had strained the muscles in her middle and lower back, or at least that's what I told her. I personally don't believe she had done anything to those muscles. I think Susan was releasing all of her hurt and frustration through her back, and making her supervisor wrong to boot. I called her supervisor to tell him that she was in too much pain to work for a few days and asked him if in the future there was any way she could avoid lifting the potato box. He said there wasn't. According to him, the box weighed thirty pounds, not seventy. If she could not lift it, she shouldn't be working there.

Susan was lucky. She quit and her back quickly improved. I

shudder to think what kind of chronic disabling back condition she might have had if she had committed herself to staying on.

I have seen this problem occur over drawers that stick, celery seedlings for transplanting that are root-bound and too hard to separate from one another, failure to pave a muddy path between greenhouses so wheeled carts are easier to push, and so on. Often management, feels the complaints are stupid or trivial. They don't see anything wrong with the equipment. They feel the employee is just whining and complaining about nothing. They don't realize the profound effect their lack of concern and inaction is having on their employee.

Anyone who's been a manager, however, knows that occasionally there will be a worker who complains about equipment that has absolutely nothing wrong with it. Such employees are irritating. Still, to be a good manager we need to rise above our gut reaction and do our best to show the employee that we take his or her complaint seriously.

Sometimes, something more sinister is going on. Sometimes management has taken a dislike to an employee and is deliberately making life miserable in order to make him or her quit. This brings us to our next syndrome.

## 12. No Way Are You Getting Rid Of Me
### (the need to be accepted)

When we are little, our parents' love is the most important thing in the world to us. When we grow up and go to work, like it or not, our bosses become our new parents in many ways. Just as having Mommy and Daddy hate us is intolerable, having our boss dislike us to the point of wanting to get rid of us is painful. Even if our employer isn't doing anything overtly to make us miserable, we can sense when our manager doesn't like us. When I conduct seminars for management, I ask the participants if any of them has ever worked for someone who disliked them. Someone always raises his or her hand. When I ask if the person cried, a woman and some-times, although rarely, a male participant will admit to crying. This kind of work situation causes the most severe and prolonged symptoms of any of the unhappy scenarios I have described.

Charlie was brought into the clinic one morning supported by two of his co-workers. The muscles in his back were contracting in painful spasms and he was unable to get comfortable in any position. The pain was so intense that he was moaning and close to tears. Because I knew he could never tolerate being X-rayed in that condition, I gave him an injection of pain medication mixed with a sedative. After it took effect, I was able to evaluate him with an exam and X-rays of his spine. The results came out negative for signs of a ruptured disc, a kidney stone, or any other serious problem. I told him he had a severe low-back strain, gave him a cold pack, loaded him up with pain relievers and muscle relaxants, and sent him home to bed.

I saw Charlie often over the next few weeks. I tried numerous different medications and physical therapy treatments in an attempt to relieve his suffering. Nothing helped. During this time, I took the opportunity to interview him.

When I asked Charlie if he liked his job, his first response was to tell me it was a good job.

But as we continued to talk, the following story gradually emerged: Charlie was a truck driver for a local trucking firm. He had worked for his present employer for a year. In his words: *I've worked my butt off for these people. I work twice as hard as all the other drivers because I drive the oldest truck in the fleet, and it's the only one that doesn't have power steering, a power tailgate release, or air conditioning. The worst part, though, is the tailgate. I've told them over and over that the tailgate sticks and is a pain to open, but they don't care. That's how this happened to me. I was yanking on that damn tailgate lever again, because it was stuck, and I hurt my back. I knew I would hurt myself, if I had to keep yanking on that thing.*

If I hadn't known better at that point, I would have concluded that Charlie was working for monstrous, hateful people who abused their workers. He obviously felt uncared for and unappreciated.

I didn't find out the rest of the story, until I called Charlie's boss. According to the boss, they had hired him after one of their best drivers, Charlie's brother, had asked them to. Charlie had previously had a drinking problem, but had been sober for some time. With some misgivings, they hired him.

Although Charlie showed up every day and did his job, they felt he had a chip on his shoulder and was too much of a loner. According to the owner, they had tried to include him, but he never fit in somehow. They always made a point of inviting him to the company picnics and softball games. He always said he would come, but something always seemed to come up at the last minute.

Even worse, they had reports that he was still drinking and, although no one at work had smelled alcohol on his breath, they felt he was a ticking time bomb. When I asked about the problem with the tailgate, the owner said they had checked it out, and it appeared to be working fine. He said yes, it can stick when the truck is loaded, but all mechanical tailgates are like that.

Then came the corker. One week before Charlie's injury, they had purchased a beautiful new truck. But instead of promoting Charlie to drive the new truck, they hired a new driver. They kept Charlie in the same old truck. In the owner's words, *Charlie is lucky to have a job. Frankly, doctor, the best thing for everybody would be if Charlie just quit. We're only keeping him on because of his brother. There's no way I'm going to trust that guy with a $150,000 piece of equipment.*

What was Charlie's pain really about? Why wouldn't it go away? Once we realize we're not just dealing with a physical body with strained muscles, but a human being whose feelings have been hurt to the core, such questions become easy to answer.

Some people quit when confronted with a situation like this. Others go to their employer and ask for an explanation. Some fight back and file a harassment suit. Others feel thoroughly miserable but keep going to work anyway because they feel they have no choice.

Many, however, respond like Charlie did. He kept going to work and tried to put the whole thing out of his mind. He resolved not to think about it or let it bother him. He actually succeeded in becoming largely unaware of how much emotional turmoil his work situation caused. Then he injured himself so badly that he never had to go back to work and face the situation again.

Despite all the best medical treatments over the next several months, Charlie's back continued to hurt him. CT and MRI scans showed no disk problem. Finally, he became so desperate to escape his pain that he agreed to try fusion surgery on his spine. That relieved his symptoms for a few weeks, but then, just before the doctor was ready to release him to go back to work, his pain returned with a vengeance. Charlie is now permanently disabled. His case cost his employer's insurance company $200,000.

Such cases are always a nightmare. I call them *death struggles*. One worker I treated believed his bosses were trying to railroad him out of the organization because he was the only honest one there, and the rest of them were stealing from the organization. Unfortunately, he stayed to fight until his emotional and physical health failed.

Another case involved an employee whose superiors came to regard him as a troublemaker and began to manipulate his work assignments and schedule in ways they knew were unpleasant for him. It was an attempt to force him to quit. He developed problems with pleurisy that prevented him from doing the job they wanted him to do.

Sometimes in such situations, the employee is difficult and the employer's feelings are understandable. On the other hand, sometimes the employer has it in for an employee for no legitimate reason. Often what's going on lies somewhere between the two extremes.

## 13. SHORT-STAFFED
### (THE NEED TO REST)

Understaffing is another common cause of illness and injury at work. In many businesses, there is simply no one else available to take up the slack when someone is off sick or on vacation. The people who are unlucky enough to be healthy are left holding the bag. Not only are they expected to do their own jobs, but those of their co-workers as well.

When morale is high, the situation doesn't usually cause illness. Most of us are willing to take on an extra burden as long as we feel our managers and co-workers are concerned about us. But when morale is low – look out. If we begin to feel like work is simply being dumped on us and nobody cares, we risk getting sick or injured.

## 14. Eight Days a Week
### (the need for rest)

This syndrome is about working overtime. Many companies have periods when business is much heavier than usual. Several large orders come in all at once and mandatory overtime is necessary. Often employees don't object to working extra hours. The pay is good, usually time-and-a-half, and they accept it as part of their job. The problem occurs when the amount of weekly overtime becomes excessive or the overtime is a matter of taking on too much. The following case is an example.

Will, a 35-year-old attorney, had been suffering from severe dizziness for three months. He had been referred by his family doctor to an ear, nose, and throat specialist, who told him, *You have benign positional vertigo, which means you're dizzy, but it's not serious.* Although he wasn't sure of exactly what was causing the problem, the doctor offered some pills. Unfortunately, this treatment would not stop the condition. Will then began searching for something he could do for himself. He started watching his diet closely and later tried acupuncture treatments. Neither worked.

When I saw Will, I told him dizziness is often a symptom of feeling overwhelmed. He told me that in his zest to become a successful attorney, he had overextended himself. His caseload was such that there simply were not enough hours in the day to adequately prepare. Will's dizziness quickly went away when he focused his attention on that problem. Part of it involved resolving to stop accepting new cases until he had his caseload under control.

Whether you are dizzy from the flu, labyrinthitis, or some other cause, once you have been to the doctor and ruled out any serious cause, you would benefit from taking the following personal inventory:

> Have I refused to allow myself to rest? Am I working too much?

> Do I feel exhausted?

☞ Am I facing something that is difficult or frightening to me?

☞ Am I faced with an impossible amount of work?

☞ Do I need a vacation?

☞ Am I experiencing a stressful situation with relatives?

☞ Has it been more than a week since I've taken any time for myself to do something I enjoy, just for the fun of it?

☞ Do I hate my job or someone at work so much that I dread going to work?

☞ Do I have a trip coming up?

If your answer to any of the above questions is *yes*, investigate further. Rather than spending more money on doctors or medicine, a one-hour visit with a family counselor would be a wise investment.

## 15. END OF THE SEASON SYNDROME
### (THE NEED FOR MONEY)

This syndrome is about the mysterious malady that seizes workers prior to layoffs. When we are laid off work, our wages stop and we are forced either to find other work or to go on unemployment. Few of us are so desperate or dishonest that we will actually fake an injury so we can collect worker's compensation. If our need for money is strong, however, our unconscious may arrange an injury for us, particularly when disability benefits are significantly higher than unemployment benefits.

Most large employers dread layoffs for this specific reason. They know that an entire year of effort in promoting safety and accident prevention can go down the drain in the last four weeks of the season. As an example, in the Salinas Valley, the growing and harvesting season runs from April through November. During November, local clinics are deluged with back injuries, strains, and sprains that drag on and on. Like it or not, being in pain from a back injury can be an effective way of keeping food on the table and a roof over our heads. Our society needs to face the fact that this happens and make some decisions as to what to do about it. Do we continue to turn a blind eye to the situation? Or can we create new incentives that lead workers toward health rather than toward disability and prolonged suffering?

## 16. WILL YOU PLEASE FIX THIS?
### (COMPLAINING ABOUT HAZARDOUS EQUIPMENT)

What happens when we report a broken or hazardous piece of equipment to our superiors and nothing is done about it?

Joe, a garbage truck driver, came into my office early one morning with a painful blister on the little toe of his right foot. *I got this because my boss wouldn't fix my accelerator pedal. It's been sticking for months. I told them over and over,* he said.

I took a scalpel and unroofed the blister, placing some soothing ointment and a Band-Aid on it. Joe and I both thought it odd, because the blister had come on suddenly that morning for no apparent reason. He had done nothing unusual and was wearing the same old comfortable pair of boots.

*Well,* I said, *you can go back to work now.*

*Oh, no,* Joe said. *There is no way I am going back there until that accelerator is fixed.*

I called Joe's boss to check on a modified job for him. He sounded guilty. *Tell Joe to take the day off – we're fixing his truck right now,* he said. *I should have taken care of it a lot sooner.*

An injury can get something fixed when nothing else can. It's a common cause of work-related injuries.

# 14 WILL YOU PLEASE SHUT UP

J anet came into my office with her ears so plugged she could hardly hear. If you've ever had one or both of your ears plugged, you know it's an aggravating feeling. You feel like you're at the bottom of a barrel. Sometimes they are just plugged with wax. In the process of cleaning our ears with Q-tips, we gradually jam the wax down in our ear canal, until it blocks the whole thing, and we have to go to the doctor to get our ears washed out.

Janet thought maybe this was her problem, but when I looked in her ears there was no wax build-up. Rather, she had a large accumulation of golden fluid behind each eardrum.

Janet had a common condition called serous otitis, an inflammation of the ear, with fluid accumulation in the little space behind the eardrum that has three little bones in it. Normally the space is filled with air. The air enters through the Eustachian tube, which connects the chamber with our nasal passages. When fluid accumulates in that space, it presses against the eardrum and muffles our hearing, just like damping a drum by filling it with water.

Serous otitis is usually not caused by infection. Sometimes tumors or blockage of the Eustachian tube bring it on, but often when we experience serous otitis, we don't even have a cold. Typically it lasts a week or two, but it can last four to six weeks or even longer.

Janet's was a typical case. She hadn't had a cold or any other problem that might have caused her ears to fill with fluid; they were plugged for no apparent reason. After explaining her condition, I put her on the usual treatment: antibiotics to cover the possibility of infection and a decongestant to try to open up the Eustachian tubes. She returned a week later, no better than before. In Janet's case, I proceeded on the assumption that her unconscious mind was filling her ears with fluid. What could her unconscious mind be trying to accomplish by doing this? To answer the question, we need to look at what affect the fluid was having on her. One, it was irritating, and two, it was interfering with her ability to hear. Might there be some need to block out something irritating that she didn't want to hear?

Janet was new in town. She told me her husband had taken a job reorganizing a branch of local government that was in shambles. The people in his department were all feuding with one another and he consistently came home complaining about the problems. Because Janet hadn't taken a job, but had elected to stay home and care for her two small children, she hadn't been out much and hadn't met many people. That left her completely dependent on her husband for her social life. Being desperate for adult contact, Janet tried her best to listen to her husband faithfully each night, after he returned home late. Unfortunately, his evening ranting sessions had been going on for two or three months by the time Janet came to me for help. Like Janet, I think many of us might build up a need to block similar situations out after awhile.

When you get to the point where part of you really doesn't want to listen, but you can't see a way out of the situation, your unconscious may start interfering with your hearing.

Rather than trying to convince Janet that it was brought on by her inability to tell her husband to keep quiet, I told her that her ears needed a rest. I told her husband he had to keep his conversations with her to a minimum, until she became better. Janet made an uneventful recovery, once she received some rest from her husband's work problems.

⟫•⟪

When we spend a lot of time on the telephone at work and start having an earache, or a plugged feeling in our telephone ear, it is often a symptom of spending too much time dealing with irritating people or situations. Often it happens when we are overworked. Sometimes we resent our managers or coworkers and our ear will become symptomatic to get us out of the office for a time. Our ear may be affected either because we're being overwhelmed by too much noxious input, as in Janet's case, or simply because it is a crucial body part that guarantees an exit from work when we've *had it* (as in the case of a receptionist).

It's easy to understand why both of Janet's ears plugged up. Her husband's voice was coming in both of them. In a similar vein, a receptionist might only have problems with her telephone ear. It's not often immediately obvious, however, why serous otitis sometimes affects one ear and not the other. When that happens, you may need to do a little detective work.

Here's an example: Phyllis, a woman in her 40s, came to see me with her right ear filled with fluid. She complained that for the past week she could hardly hear anything out of it. It was extremely irritating, because she was choir director for her church, and she had to be able to hear well in order to function.

*Does it bother you most when you direct the choir?* I asked.

*Yes, it's awful. It sounds like I'm in a barrel. I really need to be able to hear the piano, and it's gotten to the point that I can hardly hear it.*

*Which side of you is the pianist on?* I asked.

*My right side.*

*Is there any problem with the piano player?*

She looked surprised and said, *Why, as a matter of fact, our wonderful accompanist of many years resigned about two months ago. She was a pleasure to work with. She always knew the music backward and forward and never missed a note. I don't know if the new one is going to work out. She's having a problem with the music. It's been irritating working with her. She hits lots of sour notes, and her timing is off. I think I'm going to have to tell her it's not going to work out. You don't think this has anything to do with my hearing, do you?*

I told her I didn't know, but it was an interesting coincidence.

The unconscious often is very literal in handing out symptoms. When we are in painful situations, we experience painful conditions. When we are in irritating situations, we experience irritating conditions. In the two cases above, it was not necessary to have the ears hurt, only to block out the unwanted, irritating sound. Although having our ears plugged up is intensely irritating, it is a great way to vent some generic irritation that needs release.

# 15 ART SHOW SYNDROME

Most of us are very sensitive about showing our creative work to others, whether it be performing a song, reading a poem, taking a painting or sculpture to a gallery, or submitting a manuscript to a publisher. Why? We don't have to dig very deep for an answer. We're revealing our soft underparts to the critics, who are only too happy to disembowel us with their criticisms and rejections. Those of us with high self-esteem turn out our work with little difficulty. Those of us with low self-esteem feel anxious at the idea that others may dislike our creation. Having our artwork rejected seems to equate somehow with having little worth as a person. In rejection, our worst fear is realized: we are no good.

Feeling that we are no good is one of the most painful feelings a human being can have. As with most powerful negative feelings, we tend to suppress it. Thus, as our art show approaches, we feel confident. We look forward to showing our work even though this is when we are most prone to developing disturbing symptoms that may interfere with our career. It may be a psychological symptom such as *writer's block,* or it may be a physical symptom.

Bev was a brilliant young violinist, a rising star in her local community. She soon found herself concertmaster of her community orchestra. When she was in her mid-twenties, she made the decision to go on tour as a violin soloist. As preparations for her debut and national tour began, her fingers froze up. She began losing the fluid coordination that allowed her to play so brilliantly. As her technique fell apart, Bev naturally became nervous and agitated. She had to cancel her tour. She went to the best specialists, but no one could pinpoint the cause of her problem.

Sadly, Bev never sought qualified emotional help. As her playing continued to deteriorate, she went from being a prodigy to being a second-rate player. Eventually she gave up the violin entirely.

It's interesting that Bev was fine as long as she was playing in an orchestra. After all, as the concertmaster, the glare of the spotlight only shown on her for a brief moment, when she took her bow at the beginning of the performance. Then she took her seat and melted into the relative anonymity of the violin section.

The prospect of being spotlighted for an entire performance in front of a huge crowd is another matter entirely. That's enough to give anyone a bad case of the jitters. Bev, however, genuinely thought she was looking forward to her tour and was completely out of touch with the part of her that felt inadequate, exposed, and terrified. That part did what it had to do to stop her.

The above case is an example of how self-esteem issues interfere when we start putting our creative efforts out into the world. Writer's block, lack of inspiration, chronic fatigue, injuries, accidents, or other recurrent health problems that take us away from our art are common manifestations of *Art Show Syndrome*. Although she desperately wanted to believe she was looking forward to performing, she needed to ask herself the following questions:

1. What's my worst fear of how people will react to my work?
2. Whose opinion is important to me and how would I feel, if that person hated my work?
3. I know part of me thinks my work is good, but if I really look, is there a part of me that's afraid it's not? What does that part say?
4. If I were going to criticize something about my work, what would it be?
5. Can I look at myself in the mirror and say *I love you*, and mean it?
6. Do I dislike my name? Do I hate it?
7. Do I think I am homely or unattractive?

The last three questions are very revealing. They tend to reflect problems with our self-esteem. If health problems or accidents continually interfere with your attempts to pursue a career in the arts, you would be wise to see a good therapist and focus on self-esteem issues.

# 16 Things You May Not Want to Know About Sex

## I Want to Get Married...I Think

Linda, an extraordinarily beautiful and intelligent young woman in her late twenties, came to see me about a terrible case of genital herpes. She had been plagued by painful, blistering sores around the opening of her vagina for the past year. Her regular doctor, a specialist at a university medical center, was unavailable.

Herpes, as many readers are aware, is a virus that causes uncomfortable, blistery sores, commonly called cold sores. They occur most often around the edge of the lips or on the genitals, although they can occur anywhere on the body. Cold sores are usually a source of minor irritation and discomfort that heal themselves in about a week or two. While some of us may never have a cold sore, about 15 percent of the population have them anywhere from once or twice a year to nearly continuously. The virus that causes the sores can spread through kissing or through sexual relations. No one knows why some of us have them, while others appear to be immune. Many have kissed someone with a cold sore on his or her lip, but still never personally had one.

There are two common strains of the virus: Herpes Type I and Herpes Type II. They cause the same sores and both can occur anywhere on your body. Cold sores or fever blisters can be precipitated by a fever, a sunburn or windburn and, at least in some people, by stress. The medication Linda was taking helps moderate and control the outbreaks but does not cure the condition.

Hers was a worst-case scenario. She had started experiencing painful sores on the lips of her vagina about one and a half years earlier.

For the past year, she'd had active lesions nearly continuously. Hers were not some minor irritation, but were painful, burning, raw sores that interfered severely with her sex life. The medication helped slightly, but not enough.

Linda was desperate. After listening to her story, I told her I thought I could help. She wanted to overcome the herpes because she wanted to have a relationship with a man. Sexual relations at that point were out of the question. It was simply too painful. Besides, her condition was contagious and the last thing she wanted to do was give it to someone else.

Ponder for a moment the words: *Sex is simply too painful.* If we remember that our unconscious often speaks metaphorically through our body's symptoms, it might be Linda's unconscious trying to say to her through her vagina that, *I've been hurt too badly by men to be that close again. I'm still hurting too much to have intimate relations with a man.*

In a private session, I asked her the obvious question, *Did you go through any kind of a major breakup in the six months prior to the beginning of your herpes problem?*

Reluctantly, she admitted, *Yes, but I'm over that now.*

*Tell me what happened.*

*Until Barry came along, I never really let myself fall completely in love. We had a whirlwind romance and were engaged to be married. He was a graduate student I saw mainly on weekends. We were going to have a summer wedding. It would have been two years ago this coming August. Three months before the wedding, he left me. He said he had fallen in love with another woman and then he just disappeared. We never really got to talk about it.*

I paused for a moment, then said, *That must have been awful.*

*Well,* she said, *life goes on.*

*Are you sure you are really over it?*

She replied, *It's not going to do any good to think about it, so I've just done my best to go on with my life.*

*Linda,* I said, *you had your heart broken. That's one of the most painful experiences a person can endure. It may be that inside you're still hurting. Would you be willing to try hypnosis to see if there is some part of you that is making these herpes sores keep coming back in order to stop you from getting involved and being hurt again?*

Obviously skeptical, but desperate, Linda agreed. She knew she wanted to marry, and the notion that somehow her vagina didn't want her to was a bizarre notion to her.

During the first session, Linda laughed hysterically every time I started to hypnotize her. This was challenging for me — I spent the session trying to figure out whether to laugh along with her or to look stern and reproach her. I wondered if I should keep trying or try a different approach. No matter what I tried, or how hard she tried to compose herself and be serious, as soon as she closed her eyes she would collapse into uncontrollable laughter. On her way out, we set up another appointment, and I lamely told her that sometimes the unconscious causes laughter as a way of protecting a person from opening up. That, of course, set her off again.

When she returned a week later, she gave me a very sweet look and said, *Doctor, you were right about why I was laughing so much last time, and I'm going to cooperate with you today.*

I had to admire her courage. She was willing to do anything to improve her situation.

Linda went easily into a light trance, with only a few giggles. I asked to speak to the part of her that was causing the symptoms to occur and, after tears began to flow from her closed eyes, the cure quickly began. In her normal waking state, she had become walled off from her continuing grief over her broken engagement. In a light trance, with someone there to help, her grief came to the surface.

I encouraged her to dig out and express all the undealt-with pain that she had buried alive. Grief is ready for burial only when it's dead and done with. If, like Linda, we try to bury it prematurely, it festers underground.

As she connected with her grief and worked through it, she improved. Within four months, she was off the medication and the outbreaks occurred less frequently. When I last heard from her, she was having a satisfying relationship with a man, and they were talking marriage.

Intimacy is risky business. Sure it feels great to fall in love, but it hurts horribly, when it doesn't work out. Consciously, we may have the desire for love, warmth, closeness, sex, and a shared life with another. But if we have unhealed, festering wounds inside, our unconscious may step in with a heavy hand and put a stop to it.

When our unconscious wants to discourage us from intimate involvement, it tends to go for the parts of our bodies that are involved. It doesn't make our foot hurt. That wouldn't make us reluctant to have sex. It generally goes for our sex organs and other nearby parts. The symptoms are designed to make us think twice about having sex.

When our genitals act up and put a damper on our sex lives, we would be wise to sit down with a counselor and explore the negative side of our intimate relationships. How have we been hurt? Could we be frightened of being hurt again? Are we irritated at our partner? Would we prefer to avoid sex? What scares us about being deeply involved? How do we feel about losing our freedom? Would moving in with someone be expensive, messy, and complicated? Do we have doubts about how the relationship will work out in the long run?

———⯈•◯•⯇———

Let's look at another case. Remember, our unconscious mind speaks symbolically. In our society, the symbol for marriage is the wedding band.

Rosalie and I were talking at a party when she suddenly asked, *Why would this finger itch so much every time I put a ring on it? It's only that one... none of the others itch.* She had rings on several of her other fingers.

I watched her rubbing the ring finger of her left hand.

*Isn't that the finger a person puts a wedding band on?* I asked innocently.

*Yes,* she said. *It's my engagement ring.*

*Oh? How soon is the wedding?*

About a month from now. It'll be my second marriage.

*How do you feel about getting married? Any reservations?*

She gave me a funny look and nodded, *Lots.*

I smiled and raised my eyebrow. *Maybe your engagement ring is trying to send a message?*

A little smile crossed Rosalie's face as she made the connection. Two weeks later she told me she had finally worked up the nerve to break off her engagement. Rosalie's first marriage had been *hell*, as she put it, and the only reason she became engaged was because the fellow had begged her to marry him. Part of her was lonely enough to say *yes*. But she really didn't want to.

Our culture is just beginning to understand how our unconscious mind interacts not only with our bodies, but with our environment and the events in our lives as well.

A few years ago, I had a male patient who was going through a very rough period with his wife and confided in me that he was contemplating divorce. That week he went surfing, just as he'd been doing for years, and his wedding band mysteriously was swept off his finger into the ocean. If it was an accident, it was quite a coincidence. He and his wife went into counseling and made it through the crisis. Events in our lives have a way of responding to our inner needs, beliefs, and desires.

If you're developing problems with your wedding band, or if you find yourself toying with it, you might ask yourself if you are going through some unhappiness in your marriage or if you are considering divorce.

## I've Got an Itch to Scratch

Madge, a woman in her late thirties, came to see me because she was experiencing persistent itching in her vagina. She had been treated several times over the past eight months. Once or twice the doctor had told her it was a yeast infection, but several other times he couldn't find any cause. I didn't see any yeast or other signs of infection under the microscope, but prescribed a vaginal cream anyway. Madge asked if I had any idea why she kept experiencing the itching. I tested her for diabetes, as frequent yeast infections can be a sign of undiagnosed diabetes. When the test returned negative, I decided to look for a hidden issue.

I asked if the itch interfered with her sex life. She said, *No*. In fact, having sex relieved the itching.

I was a bit puzzled. I asked if there were any tensions or bad feelings between her and her husband.

She said, *No, we have a very good relationship.* She thought for a moment and then admitted she was extremely jealous and obsessed, fearing that he was running around on her. She loved him, he was nice to her, they got along, but she was so suspicious that she was almost to the point of hiring a detective to follow him around.

Isn't it remarkable what will come out, if the doctor takes a moment to ask?

I certainly didn't have any solution to her problem. All I did was listen sympathetically and tell her that such strong feelings could certainly have something to do with her vaginal itching. Madge was not really angry with her husband, because she didn't really believe he was cheating on her. She didn't need to deny him sex. On the contrary, if anything, having sex with him seemed to reassure her that he was still interested in her.

If we look at her physical symptoms as a metaphor for inner emotions, the fact that his sexual attentions felt good to her and relieved her itching goes along well with the fact that, on an emotional level, she craved his attentions. Having sex with him helped relieve her anxieties.

I saw Madge only once for that problem. About six months later, she came into my office with one of her children for some minor complaint. Afterward, I took her aside and asked how she was doing with her itching problem.

*You know, doctor, I haven't itched a day since I walked out of your office.*

Funny how just talking about something like that can cure a person.

## THE GUILTY VAGINA

Many of us feel it's wrong to have *casual sex.* It's important to us to have sex only in the context of a serious relationship – a relationship that might lead to marriage, or at least to a committed relationship. Despite the wave of sexual liberation that has swept over the Western world in the past decades, many of us still carry traditional values about the rights and wrongs of premarital sex. Even today, some young people are being raised with some pretty strong, old-fashioned values, one of them being that it's wrong for a young woman to have sex before marriage, period.

When our sex glands call for a *romp in the hay,* they may collide with deeply imbued values. When symptoms occur, they have two purposes: to try to stop us from continuing to violate our values or to ventilate some of our unconscious shame and guilt. I'll explain what I mean with some examples.

Michelle, 19, came to see me because she was having a lot of burning and irritation in her vagina. This had been going on for two or three months and was making sexual relations uncomfortable. Her examination and lab tests were unremarkable. I told her she may have some kind of minor infection, and I would give her some medication. At that, she earnestly asked me why she had the problem and why it had lasted so long.

*Michelle, did you know that sometimes a woman could have a lot of vaginal problems, if she's feeling uncomfortable in some way about sexual relations?*

*Really? That's funny because I'm engaged, and well... we've both been trying not to have sex, until we're married. But we've been doing it anyway. We're both members of the same church, and we believe people really shouldn't have sex before marriage.*

*When are you planning to get married?*

*Not for two more years.*

*Two years! That's a long time to wait.*

She went on to explain all the reasons they had to wait.

There's a high probability that Michelle's vaginal discomfort was a physical expression of her inner discomfort about sex before marriage. I didn't see Michelle again, but I hope our conversation eased her conflict enough to clear up her problem.

Closely related to those kinds of guilty feelings are the feelings of betrayal that some widows get when they attempt to become sexually active, after the loss of their husband. Many women find themselves caught in a bind between their need for love, sex, and companionship on the one hand, and the feeling they are betraying their lifelong partner on the other. Sometimes, the fear of losing another mate contributes to the conflict. Even when enough time has passed for it to be considered socially appropriate, when it comes time to go to bed, painful or irritating vaginal symptoms may occur. The symptoms usually go away once the widow's tender feelings are discussed openly and the conflicts are worked through.

In summary, guilt over sexual expression tends to express itself in women as vaginal pain, pelvic pain, infections, odors and irritation.

In men, it manifests itself as penile pain, rashes, discharge, and irritation. This brings us to our next hidden issue.

## THE GUILTY PENIS

People catch syphilis, gonorrhea, chlamydia, trichomonas, herpes, AIDS, crab lice, and venereal warts from having sexual relations with each other. These are real diseases that require antibiotics or other forms of medical treatment and, of course, can be caught independently of any emotional factors. But what about the man who goes to see the doctor for a discharge from his penis a week or two after a sexual transgression and the tests for venereal disease are negative?

The condition is called non-specific urethritis (NSU) or non-gonococcal urethritis. They mean the same thing – inflammation of the urethra (the tube that we urinate through) caused by something other than gonorrhea. Often, no cause can be found.

Tom came to see me for a penile discharge. He was anxious and fearful he'd given it to his wife. He had just spent an entire week sleeping with one of his old girlfriends whom he'd run into at an out-of-town business meeting. He had enjoyed every minute he'd been with her, but he began suffering guilt pangs on his way home.

When he got home, he did his best to put it out of his mind. Two days later, he panicked when he developed a penile discharge. He had already made love to his wife and was terrified he might have given her a venereal disease. He was caught in an awful dilemma — tell her and risk his marriage or deceive her and risk destroying her reproductive organs.

I tested him for disease, the results of which were all negative, and started him on the time-honored treatment for NSU – 100 mg of doxycycline twice a day. His main concern was whether he should tell his wife. He agonized over it. He even considered getting some extra medicine and sneaking it into her food. I told him I wouldn't participate in that.

After a week on the drug he improved, but two or three days before the medicine ran out, the discharge began again. I put him back on medication for another ten days and continued to help him work through his guilt feelings. Tom finally decided to face the music and tell his wife. Their marriage weathered the storm with the help of some counseling. She took some medicine just in case, although she, too, tested negative for any sexually transmitted disease. Guilt feelings about sexual transgressions often manifest themselves as penile discharges that defy diagnosis or treatment. Our guilty feelings convert into a feeling that we are contaminated.

Generally, these feelings of shame, debasement, and guilt manifest themselves as a lot of anxiety about sex and a penile discharge that comes and goes for a few weeks to a few months. In severe cases, it can lead to chronic bodily pains that defy diagnosis and treatment.

I took care of a man who had chronic pains in his chest muscles and upper abdomen. They had started a few years before, shortly after he had ended a prolonged affair with a woman, who worked in his office. He had lived out all his sexual fantasies with the woman, but couldn't bring himself to leave his wife and children for her. Eventually his wife found out, and he was forced to give up his mistress. Years later, he still felt lustful every time he looked at his former mistress. At the same time, he regarded himself as the lowest form of life on earth for what he had put his wife through.

Compounding his self-hate was the fact that since his affair had ended, he would periodically go on drunken debaucheries with prostitutes and more or less make a fool of himself publicly. He simply could not forgive himself for those things, even after he'd sworn off booze and prostitutes.

Psychotherapeutic practitioners believe that terrible self-hate and self-flagellation often lead to very real physical pains. It's almost as if we are physically beating ourselves up, leaving our bodies painfully bruised. I sent this man to an excellent specialist, who agreed with my diagnosis: fibromyalgia, painful muscles of unknown cause. The clinical diagnosis was based on a history of chronic muscular pains without positive physical findings. There were no abnormalities on any laboratory tests. We did an exhaustive and very expensive medical work-up, including blood tests, ultrasound examinations, intestinal X-rays, and CT scans. All were normal.

The case clearly illustrates the inadequacies of our current medical model. The terrible guilt the man carried is never going to come to the surface in a normal appointment with a doctor. In our present medical model, it's a more appropriate topic for a visit with his priest. Why would the patient ever bring something like that up, when the focus of the examination is on finding something wrong with his body?

## THE ANGRY VAGINA

Agnes, a 32-year-old woman, was having problems with recurring vaginal infections. For four months she had a reoccurring, bad-smelling vaginal discharge. I was the third doctor she had seen. The other two doctors both gave her various antibiotics for the minor infection. The medicines had temporarily relieved the problem, but it kept coming back. I took specimens from her vagina, which showed only nonspecific inflammation.

*Agnes,* I said, *when this started, were you going through anything uncomfortable with your husband?*

She looked surprised. *Why yes, as a matter of fact I was.*

*Was he cheating on you?*

She looked shocked as she nodded. *Yes. Could that have anything to do with this? My problem did start up right about that time.*

*I don't know,* I said. *Are you over it?*

She shook her head. *No, I'm not. He lied to me about it at first. He finally admitted he was running around on me when it became obvious to him that I knew about it. I just don't trust him anymore. He could be cheating on me right now.*

I explained to Agnes that these angry, uncomfortable feelings could certainly manifest themselves as vaginal problems, even in the absence of any sexually transmitted diseases he might be bringing home.

*Tell me, doctor,* she said, *could this also make my face break out? I haven't had pimples since I was in high school, but the last two or three months my face has been breaking out like crazy.*

Her pimples might have been a coincidence, but I think it is quite likely they had something to do with the very major problem she was having in her marriage. I urged her to see a marriage counselor with her husband, and if he refused, to go by herself.

Anger at our partners can cause not only unpleasant symptoms affecting our genitals, as in Agnes's case, but it can also cause problems with other organs in the general vicinity of our intimate parts.

## I Won't Admit it, Doctor, but I'm Pissed!

Apparently the bladder is close enough to the vagina that it is affected by irritations that build up in our intimate relationships.

Gladys, a 50-year-old woman, had an average of five or six bladder infections a year. Whenever I looked at her urine under the microscope, it was brimming with white blood cells and bacteria. After a full course of antibiotics, she would more or less recover, but she would often still have some low-grade burning or discomfort, even when she had no overt bladder infection.

One of the principles of the relationship between the mind and the body that bears repeating is that *the more resistant we are to talking about our inner feelings, the more forcefully the dammed-up emotions will drive symptoms out into the body.* Sure enough, Gladys vigorously resisted when I attempted to talk to her about the possibility that her symptoms might be caused by chronic marital irritations. At first, she insisted everything in her life was fine and that her problem was an infection and not any kind of mental problem.

Over time she opened up. Sadly, she was living with a husband she hated. He was an abusive alcoholic who apparently hated her just as much, and they were locked in a marital feud that was a duel to the death. She hated him, but she was too frightened and insecure to leave him. In spite of his abusiveness, the relationship fulfilled powerful needs. And I'm sure the same applied to her husband. Why else would anyone stay in a living hell and not do anything about it? I lost track of Gladys and unless my advice to get involved in Al-Anon and counseling had some delayed effect, I'm sure she is still experiencing bladder infections. It still hurts me to watch a patient go through such seemingly pointless suffering.

---

Bladder infections and vaginal yeast infections in women are commonly associated with resentment toward their sexual partner.

Ladies, did you ever try having sex while you're in the middle of a raging bladder infection? Or with a painful vaginal infection? Usually it's pretty much out of the question – it simply hurts too much. Such infections force us to back away from intimate contact. They make it easier to say *no*. It can be hard to say *no* without one. Then we might have to risk talking about what it is that is making us angry.

Once again, it is important to emphasize that it can be difficult to distinguish between infections that have a purely physical cause and those that are emotionally induced. Sometimes a woman will experience a yeast infection after taking antibiotics or because she has undiagnosed diabetes.  In cases like these, the symptoms have nothing to do with her intimate life. A visit to the doctor's office is an important first step.

## HANDS OFF THESE BEAUTIFUL BREASTS

Breast implants are a common and popular form of cosmetic surgery. Most women who undergo the procedure do it because they want to have a beautiful figure, so they can feel better about themselves.

There is a problem though. A beautiful bosom not only makes a woman feel good about herself, it often also attracts men. What happens if a woman thinks she is ready for all that male attention, but deep down inside is uncomfortable with it?

Paula was in the process of rejecting her third set of breast implants. It was as if there was some part of her that just didn't want her to have nice, large, attractive breasts. When she asked me why it was happening to her, I guessed it would be related to conflicts concerning her relationships with men.  I asked her if there was a part of her that might be angry or disenchanted with men. She looked surprised, but said she was working through her anger toward men with a therapist. She was amazed I would zero in on that without knowing anything about her.

Once we understand how the unconscious uses the body to express its needs, connections like this one become obvious. Paula was unhappy with her small breasts and wanted to enlarge them so she would be happier with the way she looked. Meanwhile, her unconscious actually hated men, or was frightened of them and couldn't bear the idea of being intimately fondled by them. This part of her desperately needed her breasts to be small, so men wouldn't come knocking on her door.

I'm not saying that all small-breasted women need to avoid men. Breast size appears to be genetically inherited and has nothing to do with our emotions and needs. Many large-breasted women are not comfortable with close male relationships. And, many small-breasted women have completely normal relationships with men, while others receive breast implants and have no problem with them.

While it's purely conjecture on my part that Paula's emotional conflicts could have made her reject the implants, I thought it was important enough to discuss with her. Whenever you have negative physical reactions to medical treatments, you would be wise to look for a part of yourself that feels negatively about some aspect or consequence of the treatments. Theoretically, if Paula can work through her conflicts, she should be able tolerate the implants, or at least become more comfortable with herself the way she is.

## NOT TONIGHT, HONEY, I HAVE WARTS

So far, we've seen angry, guilty, and hurt genitals that helped people avoid intimate relations. There is another reason that we might want to avoid intimate relations – sometimes our partner doesn't turn us on.

Genital warts, or condylomata, is another common genital infection. These ugly little guys can get on the skin and mucous membranes of the penis or vagina, and anywhere else around the genitals for that matter. They are clearly caused by a virus, one of the human papilloma viruses, and can be spread from person to person, although many people don't seem to catch them, even when exposed repeatedly.

The usual treatment is to burn them off with either electric current or chemical treatments, or to freeze them off with liquid nitrogen. Unless they are huge, their removal normally poses little problem, and they don't usually come back.

John, a young married man of 30, came to see me because of several small warts on his penis. I gave him a little local anesthetic and burned them with the electric needle. I told him to check back with me in a few weeks if he had any recurrence, and to be sure to have his wife checked by her gynecologist.

He came in four weeks later with another crop of tiny warts on his penis. I asked him if his wife had seen her doctor, and he said she'd been given a clean bill of health. I questioned him closely as to whether either of them had been unfaithful, and he assured me that nothing like that had happened. I checked his hands to make sure he didn't have a *mother wart* on them that was somehow seeding the ones on his penis. There were none.

John resignedly climbed up on the table and I cooked every last little tiny excuse for a wart, making sure this time that I got them all.

Five weeks later he came back in with yet another crop. By now he was beseeching me to tell him why it was happening, and whether he was going to have to go through the humiliation of clinic visits once a month for the rest of his life.

At that point I felt discouraged, so I packed John off to a urologist to see if he had any magic for those warts.

I didn't hear from John for four months. Then one day he reappeared and said, *Dr. Retherford, would you mind if I came back to you? I saw the specialist you sent me to, but he's just doing the same thing you are, and frankly, I think you were doing a better job.*

I said I would take him back. We went through our little ritual with the electric needle once again. As I stood up and prepared to go, John sat upon the examining table and said something that struck a chord in me.

*Doctor, these things are really starting to get to me. They're making me feel like I don't even want to have sex with my wife anymore.* Once again the unconscious was blurting out the truth via a bodily symptom: *I don't even want to have sex with my wife anymore.*

I sat back down and said, *John, you know, sometimes symptoms like this can come up when there's tension in a marriage. Is there anything wrong between you and your wife?*

*Not really,* he said, frowning slightly. *Nothing serious anyway. You know... the usual minor irritations.*

*Sometimes our hands will start hurting when we're doing a job we don't want to be doing,* I said. *In the same way, believe it or not, sometimes people will develop ongoing problems with their genitals, if they don't feel comfortable having sexual relations with someone. How did you feel about sex with your wife before you got these warts?*

John looked puzzled and said, *That's funny, because I've never really been very turned on to my wife sexually. We've been married two years, and now I'm wondering why I married her. The girl I was going with before I met my wife really lit my fire... We had great sex together.*

Here's a man who one minute earlier told me in all sincerity that he and his wife didn't have any serious problems. I said, *It sounds like you're having some pretty serious doubts about this relationship.*

He looked at me and said, *I guess I am. I didn't really realize it until just now.*

This is a case where recurrent genital warts seemed to be the unconscious mind's way of helping a person solve a problem. How much easier it is to say to your wife as she cuddles up with you, *Not tonight, honey, I'm afraid I might give you warts,* as opposed to, *I'm sorry, dear, but I simply don't find you attractive.*

I am not advocating bringing people to tears by bluntly telling them they don't turn you on. There are many ways the subject can be broached in a sensitive manner – *You know, honey, for some reason I just haven't been very turned on sexually lately, and I'm worried about it. How about you?*

Chemistry varies, and couples have to adjust to the facts of life. Bringing it out in the open and talking about it is an important first step. We may find our partner feels the same way about us. It is best done with a sensitive therapist present to guide the interaction so it remains a productive one. We're always so afraid of saying the awful truth to our loved ones, but when it finally comes out, we usually find out they knew it all along. Saying it out loud can be the beginning of talking it out and dealing with it. That releases the energy and allows symptoms to go away.

John entered counseling with his wife, and I'm happy to report his warts went away.

## Section III

# You Can Unlock The Door to Permanent Wellness

# 17 WHERE TO START?

This part of the book is about getting better. Actually, the process of getting better started by just reading about the various hidden issues, and perhaps seeing yourself in one or more of them. It is an eye-opening experience when you realize for the first time that a past illness or injury actually helped you in some way. It allows you to look back through your life at the various times you have been sick or injured and see how your symptoms may have allowed you to postpone a trip, avoid a competition, or get out of a job you hated.

Becoming aware that hidden issues have worked on you behind the scenes is very important. Without that understanding, you are powerless to do anything except blindly repeat your patterns. Once you're aware of what's going on, you can make a decision to change.

Unfortunately, even when you understand, it's not easy to spot a hidden issue, when you are sick or injured. But, by knowing that your defenses blind you, you can make the decision to seek help from a trained professional.

## CHOOSING A THERAPIST

Ideally, your doctor should be trained not only to diagnose and treat your physical problems, but also to identify and treat any emotional factors behind your illness. While some doctors make a pretty good attempt at that, they often fall short because of time constraints, inadequate training, or patient resistance. Unless you find a doctor who is skilled and willing to take the time to look for hidden issues, you are going to be on your own. Usually you will need to find a therapist to help.

Here's where you'll reach your next stumbling block. You don't know whom to see. And even if you did, you don't want to go, don't have time, and/or can't afford it. After all, only crazy people see counselors and you know your problem is physical, not mental. Besides, you don't really need it. You can figure it out yourself. And so on. Some combination of these excuses comes up with almost everyone.

Assuming you do get past these things, there are other problems. Should you see a psychiatrist (M.D.), a psychologist (Ph.D. or MA), a social worker (L.C.S.W.), a marriage and family counselor (M.F.C.C.), a hypnotherapist, or a counselor affiliated with your church? Should you go to a counseling center or see someone in private practice? And what kind of therapy should you get? Do you need psychoanalysis for your back pain? Or is inner child work, gestalt therapy, rational-emotive therapy, or process-oriented therapy better? Are your codependence issues causing your problem, and what kind of therapist deals with those? Maybe you need a twelve-step program? Should you take antidepressants, tranquilizers, or other mood-altering medications? Maybe a psychic would help? Or a body worker?

There are a myriad of different approaches to counseling and psychotherapy, and several different types of licensed professionals to choose from. What you need to remember is that it's the person, not the degree or the particular discipline, that's most important. Ask yourself if your therapist seems to genuinely care about you. This is crucial.

Second in line of importance is the question of whether you feel you can talk easily to him or her. Good therapy comes from the heart, not from the left brain. A person can have very impressive credentials, yet be cold and clinical. A person like that will rarely do you any good. Conversely, some very fine therapists have relatively little training in psychoanalytic theory or other disciplines, yet help their clients enormously. As in many other fields, it's a combination of heart and good training that produces a skilled professional.

The first ingredient in a successful therapeutic relationship is the chemistry between you and your therapist. If this is present, conversation will very likely flow naturally to the areas where you are experiencing problems, and in due course, your hidden issues will hopefully surface and be successfully addressed.

If you decide to consult a therapist because of a physical complaint, like headaches, a rash, or shoulder pains, chances are you're not going to feel either anxious or depressed. You will probably say, *Everything's fine except for this pain.* You're not aware of any problems. This means your therapist must dig in order to bring your hidden issue to the surface. Some therapists do this well, others don't.

You cannot assume your therapist has the experience to quickly zero in on your hidden issue. In fact, some therapists might be fooled by your placid exterior, and after interviewing you, agree with you that *yes, everything does seem to be okay and you need to see a doctor for your complaints.* While most experienced therapists can avoid this pitfall, they in turn might be unclear exactly how to proceed because of lack of experience with mind-body interactions. And, if the therapist doesn't press the inquiry in the right direction, things might go off on the wrong track for a time.

The danger is that your hidden issue will remain buried as you go off on one tangent after another. I suggest that when you go to a therapist for a physical problem, you do a little homework first. While it may not always be possible for you to actually identify your hidden issue, you can narrow the search down to a few likely areas.

To help you do this, I've made up a guide you can use either by yourself, or jointly with your counselor. The guide is intended to synthesize the material presented throughout this book into a practical, usable form that you can apply to your own life. The guide will help you and your therapist focus on likely areas to explore in the hunt for hidden issues.

# 18 GOING HUNTING: A GUIDE TO HIDDEN ISSUES

How do we decide when to go hunting for a hidden issue? It's easy. Injuries or illnesses driven by hidden issues usually have certain characteristics that separate them from purely physical problems. Let me lay them out for you here.

- The pain is out of proportion to the injury.
- The illness or injury drags on longer than it should.
- We are worried about missing something because of the problem.
- The symptom makes us irritable.
- The symptom makes us feel like crying.
- The symptom exhausts us.
- The symptom makes us unable to function.
- The symptom embarrasses us.
- The symptom makes us miss a lot of school or work.
- We suddenly became accident-prone.
- For no apparent reason, the symptom comes on suddenly and violently.
- The doctor's treatments don't help or are temporary.
- The doctor can't tell us what is wrong with us.

## LOOKING FOR CLUES

The next step is to do what a good detective does and look for clues. Clues fall into eight general categories:

1. The Nature Of The Symptom
2. The Timing Of The Symptom (to correspond with the day's or week's events)
3. The Context Of The Symptom (with regard to major events or transitions in our lives)
4. How The Symptom Affects Our Ability To Do Things
5. How The Symptom Affects Those Around Us
6. How The Symptom Makes Us Feel
7. The Body Part Involved
8. The Nature Of Our Thoughts, Fears And Beliefs

You can often uncover your hidden issue by answering a few questions under each of these categories. Although you find that you are asked some of the same, or similar questions under different categories, please try to answer them all.

## CLUE No. 1:
## THE NATURE OF THE SYMPTOM

Physical symptoms, as you have already seen, can sometimes be a metaphorical expression of inner feelings. For instance, if someone hurts your feelings and you deny it, the pain can come out as actual body pain. Physical pain corresponds to emotional pain, itching to emotional irritation, physical restlessness to emotional restlessness, and so on.

For example, if someone teases you or a boss has it in for you, this can create physical pain, most often in the chest area (heartache), which can also bring you to tears.

Now, answer the following questions looking for hidden issues. Pay special attention to relationships, personal problems and work. Consider each question carefully and look for details you didn't realize were bothering you. Hidden feelings are usually the culprit.

### A.    Pain (Look for emotional pain)

&#x22A2; Has anyone been mean to you lately? Did they ridicule or tease you?

&#x22A2; Have you been critical of yourself for something you said or did?

&#x22A2; Were you not invited to a party that everyone else went to? Do you feel unpopular? Would that bother you, if you let it?

☞ Have you ended a relationship? Could you be hurting inside?

☞ Have you been wounded in love recently?

☞ Do you hate your marriage?

☞ Do you hate your job or some aspect of it? Were you by-passed for promotion? Did being bypassed hurt you? Would it bother you if you let it?

☞ Have you performed poorly at some sports activity? Would that bother you, if you let it?

## B.    Lack of Energy or Weakness (Look for emotional exhaustion)

☞ Are you driving yourself to make money? To buy something? To pay off something?

☞ Do you drive yourself because you don't feel you are good enough?

☞ Are you thinking of taking on a challenge that involves a lot of responsibility?

☞ Are you thinking of expanding your business?

☞ Do you have too much to do and not enough time to do it?

☞ As a single parent, do you have enough time for yourself?

☞ Are you working too much overtime? Are you working two jobs? Going to school and working?

☞ Have you been working and playing too hard? Do you have any free time?

☞ Are you uncomfortable being in charge? Would you be more comfortable in a job where you don't have to be an expert?

☞ Do you have conflicting feelings about your career?

☞ Are you mentally exhausted from conflicting feelings about your relationship?

## C.    Dizziness (Look for ways you are emotionally overwhelmed)

☞ Have you had too many visitors lately? Too many relatives?

☞ Have you had too much responsibility thrust on you?

☞ Do you need some peace and quiet? Is your life too compli-cated? How?

☞ Are things going too fast in your love life?

☞ Are you hopelessly behind in your work? Have you taken on too much? Is it time to get rid of some responsibilities?

## D.    Itching (look for irritation)

☞ Has somebody done something that you find irritating? Do you find your spouse irritating? Your kids? Your in-laws? Your boyfriend? Your girlfriend? Your boss?

☞ Who irritates you at work? What do they do or say?

## E.    Blindness, Deafness (suppression of inner experience)

☞ Are you suppressing some disturbing inner vision or voices?

☞ Do you have disturbing, recurrent dreams that intrude on your waking thoughts? Do you have a critical inner voice that you are trying to suppress? Are you able to suppress it?

☞ Do you habitually suppress thoughts, memories, desires, sights, sounds, or feelings?

## F.    Feelings of Pressure or Congestion (Look for congested, pressurized, subconscious feelings)

☞ Are your feelings building to the bursting point? What would bother you, if you let it?

☞ What are the minor irritations in your life? What is imperfect about your life?

### CLUE NO. 2:
### THE TIMING OF THE SYMPTOM IN REGARD TO THE DAY'S OR WEEK'S EVENTS

When does the symptom occur? Weekends? When you travel? Before you travel? On the way to work? On the way home? If a definite pattern seems to exist, it may be a tip-off to a hidden issue. Again ask yourself the questions here as they relate to day-to-day stresses.

## Does Your Symptom:

⟶ Become intense on workday mornings and diminish during the day?

⟶ Make you so uncomfortable you have to leave work early? Flare up Sunday afternoon or evening?

⟶ Come on when you are assigned a particular job?

(If you answered yes to any of the above, look for unhappiness at work.)

⟶ Come at the end of the workday? On the way home? (Look for unhappiness at home.)

⟶ In the evening or at bedtime? (Look for unhappiness in sex or intimacy.)

⟶ Come on in bed or during the night? (Look for inner emotions trying to surface.)

⟶ Come on during a particular activity? Driving? Sports? (Look for unhappiness in that activity.)

⟶ Occur just before you made a trip? (Look for a problem or anxiety involving the trip.)

⟶ Occur during periods of inactivity? Sitting around? Standing in line? (Look for some situation in the big picture of your life that makes you feel trapped.)

## CLUE NO. 3:
### THE INJURY OCCURS ABOUT THE TIME OF SOME MAJOR TRANSITION OR EVENT

In the day-to-day hustle and bustle, we often lose sight of the big picture. We go through times that are relatively smooth, and times that involve major changes or transitions. Those changes or transitions often trigger powerful emotions. If we lose touch with the feelings, an illness, accident, or injury can occur.

Somewhere between the ages of 12 and 16 we become interested in the opposite sex. We go through the stresses of dating, falling in love, being popular or unpopular, and rejection. Between the ages of 18 and 25, we start to become independent. We move from dependence on our parents to caring for ourselves – this means the first full-time job, rent, car payments, insurance, and so on. We may marry and have children. As we move into and through adulthood, eventually we face retirement.

The ground swells are difficult to spot, except in retrospect. In looking for clues, step back and consider what you were going through at about the time your symptoms started. Had you just moved to a new town? Graduated and taken your first job? Had you just retired or are you getting ready to retire?

Here are the questions to consider:

**Did Your Symptom:**

- Occur about the time you left friends behind? Did you have to leave an intimate relationship or someone you loved? Did it happen when you attempted to develop a new circle of friends?
- Occur after a move? Are you homesick?
- Occur about the time you took your first job? When you had to go through a job change? When you assumed new work responsibilities?
- Start about the time you began dating or started dating again?
- Occur about the time you went away to college or when you returned from a vacation?
- Start 1-2 months before your wedding?
- Begin about the time you had a baby? Felt the pressure of being a new parent? Occur when you had to juggle your baby's needs and your job? Or your baby's needs and your need to have time for yourself?
- Start shortly after you got married? Start when you found it difficult to adjust to marriage?
- Occur when you were in a difficult living situation?
- Start when you became engaged?
- Start about the time you finalized your divorce? Are you angry and hurt inside? Has the adjustment been difficult?
- Start after you lost a parent? Do you have hidden feelings about this? Grief? Guilt? Fear of dying or living alone?

☞ Start one to two years before you could retire? Were you burned out and needed to retire early? Do you want to start a new business?

☞ Start after you retired? Do you not know what to do with yourself?

## CLUE NO. 4:
## THE SYMPTOM AFFECTS YOUR ABILITY TO DO THINGS

This set of clues concerns symptoms that help us avoid problems in our life. For instance, does your symptom keep you from going to work? To school? Or on a trip? Does it interfere with your sex life? Or a family visit? Remember, our unconscious often creates disabling or bothersome symptoms to get us out of an unpleasant or frightening potential problem. When you say to yourself, *I need to get over this illness or injury because...,* the answer often points to the area causing trouble.

When you engage in this kind of search, keep in mind that you are looking for an opposite feeling. For instance, you might feel that you are worried about a painful ankle keeping you out of an athletic competition. You really want to compete, but inside you are dreading some aspect of the competition, which may be what is causing the problem. A symptom that keeps you from going on a date may mask the fact that you don't want to go on that date for any number of reasons. Or a symptom that keeps you from attending a social event may well mask the fact that you dread going.

This is highly charged emotional material. Once you become aware of what has been bothering you, you can ventilate your feelings with a friend or a counselor and often defuse the feelings.

For the following questions, when you answer *yes*, you need to further pinpoint it by answering additional questions about your work, school, sports, relationships, sex life, and social engagements.

### Does Your Symptom:

☞ Keep you from going to work? Keep you from doing a particular job or activity? Keep you from advancing your career?

- Keep you from going to school or handling any particular activity at school?
- Keep you from going on a trip?
- Prevent you from keeping a business engagement?
- Stop you from keeping a social engagement or cause you to postpone a conversation you were planning to have with someone?
- Keep you from going on a trip or interfere with a family visit?
- Make it difficult to participate in any athletic activity or event?
- Make you cancel a date? Or interfere with your sex life? Interfere in any way with your creative work, including exhibiting or performing it?

## EXPLORING THE YES ANSWERS

You now need to explore the areas in which you answered *yes*, in No. 4 above. To this end, please answer the following additional questions:

### FOCUSING ON WORK

- Is something bothering you at work? Is someone treating you unfairly? Has someone been rude or mean to you at work? Do you dislike someone there?
- Are you planning to confront someone? Are your complaints being ignored or belittled? Does your boss have it in for you? Have you been left in charge recently? Is your workplace short-staffed?
- Is the work environment too hot or too cold? Does it smell bad? Is it physically uncomfortable?
- Do you have enough time off to relax or to be with your family?
- Are you picking up the slack for lazy workers? Do you have to work more than one job? Are you facing a deadline?
- Have you been accused of doing something you didn't do?
- Do you feel your job is beneath you? Are you looking for another job? Why? Are you unhappy with your work hours?
- Have you been disciplined unfairly? Did someone steal your idea and get credit?

↪ Are you expected to do something that is too difficult or to lift items that are too heavy?

## FOCUSING ON SCHOOL

↪ Do you hate school? Why? Is someone calling you names or being mean or teasing you at school?

↪ Is a bully after you? Are you being humiliated? Do you feel unpopular?

↪ Did your illness make you miss a test? Do you have a low or failing grade in any classes? Are you behind in any of your classes?

↪ Does one of your teachers have it in for you? Did your illness or injury make you miss tryouts of any kind?

## FOCUSING ON A TRIP

↪ Are you dreading some aspect of an upcoming trip? Is there anything about the trip that concerns you? What? Has something come up that makes it awkward to go on the trip at this time? What could be frightening or unpleasant about this trip?

↪ Will you have to be with people you find unpleasant? Will you have to talk to someone about a painful or embarrassing experience?

↪ Are you afraid of catching a disease? Are you frightened of being mugged or having something stolen? Are you afraid of being arrested or put in jail?

↪ Are you frightened of flying? Are you apprehensive about traveling alone? Are you afraid of the heat or the cold?

## FOCUSING ON ATHLETICS OR A SPORTS EVENT

↪ Are you exercising because you think you should? How do you feel about exercising? Does your weight or build embarrass you? Do you push yourself to exercise? Does some part of you dislike exercise?

↪ Does your injury prevent you from competing?

↪ Deep inside, are you afraid of losing? Are you afraid of being humiliated or injured? Are you burned out? Have you passed your peak in this sport?

☞ Is it painful to lose to people you could have beaten a few years ago? Are you in over your head? Did some painful or negative experience happen when you were exercising or competing?

☞ Are you worried about the heat?

☞ Do you participate in this sport just for fun? Do you care whether you win or lose? Are you kidding yourself that losing doesn't bother you?

## FOCUSING ON SOCIAL ENGAGEMENTS

☞ Does part of you dread this social engagement or part of it?

☞ Are you tired of going to events you don't enjoy just to please your spouse, boyfriend, girlfriend or family member? Can you talk about it? Do you become uncomfortable from irritation, boredom, or anxiety?

☞ Did someone snub you at a party? Does your symptom help you retaliate?

☞ Do you feel uncomfortable with or left out of your spouse's family?

☞ Do you have to give a speech? Do you hate being conspicuous in any way? Do you feel nervous about it?

☞ Have you been going out too much lately? Do you feel the need for a quiet evening at home?

☞ Is being sick the only way to get out of your engagement or date? Do you intend to keep using your illness as your excuse?

## FOCUSING ON YOUR SEX LIFE

☞ Are you angry or irritated at your partner and want to get back at him or her? Do you want to punish your partner by withholding sex? Is your partner placing too many sexual demands on you?

☞ Is sex a chore for you? Would you rather avoid it? Are you fed up with this relationship but haven't the nerve to leave?

☞ Is your partner unattractive to you? Too fat? Too thin? Too smelly? Are you too embarrassed to talk about it?

➣ Do you consider your partner an inept lover but can't bring yourself to discuss your sex life?

➣ Do you feel it's wrong to have sex?

➣ Are you afraid of getting pregnant, yet part of you wants to?

➣ Do you think it is wrong to practice birth control?

➣ Are you afraid of giving someone a sexual disease or afraid of catching one yourself?

➣ Did your partner cheat on you? Are you still hurt and angry?

➣ Did you cheat on him or her and feel guilty about it? Do you feel guilty about seeing a prostitute?

## CLUE NO. 5:
## HOW SYMPTOMS AFFECT THOSE AROUND YOU

This set of symptoms helps you by serving to control and manipulate others. The symptoms can help you with a power struggle or help you prove you are right. An injury, for instance, might convince the boss that he should have fixed the piece of equipment you complained was going to hurt someone.

## DOES YOUR SYMPTOM:

➣ Show your spouse that you are right? Does it prove that it is not all in your head? Does this let you say, I told you so?

➣ Cause your spouse to give you attention and concern?

➣ Get you sympathetic attention from family and friends?

➣ Does this attention fill a need for close contact?

➣ Do you like talking about your illness to others? Does your symptom preoccupy you and help you avoid facing things you are afraid of? What?

➣ Make your boss take your complaint seriously? Will it make him fix some piece of equipment? Did you have to injure yourself to get him to listen to you?

➣ Help you win a power struggle at work? Make your coworkers feel guilty? Will things be better now?

☞ Help you with a power struggle at home? Would you have trouble saying *no* without your symptom?

☞ Cause others to pitch in and help? Is this the only way you can obtain help?

## CLUE NO. 6:
## HOW THE SYMPTOM MAKES YOU FEEL

Often symptoms make us feel bad or sad, yet we are unaware of what those feelings mean. Clue No. 1 substituted physical pain for emotional pain (i.e. chest pains subbing for hurt feelings). With Clue No. 6 we want to look at the emotional *reaction* to the symptom, rather than the actual nature of the symptom itself. Use the complete-the-sentence method here.

*My cough (headache, chest pain and so forth) makes me feel___.* For instance, *I need to cough something up, but I can't, I feel frustrated.* Sometimes you may feel like you are about to burst. Sometimes a physical pain brings you to tears. You feel sad. These are the feelings you need to become aware of. They are difficult clues to work with, since the feelings you are suppressing do not always correlate with your symptoms. For example, if you have a low-back pain stemming from a hidden issue involving resentment toward your boss, your emotional reaction may well be one of fear that your back pain will disable you forever. You're furious at your boss and need to stay away from work, but your back pain doesn't make you mad. It is too strongly suppressed. Instead it makes you afraid that you can't go back to work.

Because of that, you have to be careful about your conclusions. Still, your emotional reactions to your symptoms can be revealing and help point the way to your hidden issue. In order to explore this, I have prepared the following list of questions:

## DOES YOUR SYMPTOM MAKE YOU:

☞ Feel irritable? What might you be angry about inside? Does it make you want to get away from people? Have you had it with the people at work? Or with your spouse?

☞ Feel like you need to cry? What are you feeling sad about?

☞ Have your feelings been hurt lately? Would they have been hurt, if you let them?

☞ Feel depressed? In what way?

☞ Feel exhausted? Are you so tired that you can't function? Have you been pushing too hard?

☞ Feel trapped? Sick? Nauseated? Are you in a sickening situation?

☞ Feel like you want to die or that you are going to burst? What may be building up inside you? Sit with that bursting feeling.

☞ Feel like a failure? How?

## DOES YOUR SYMPTOM:

☞ Scare you? Are you afraid it's cancer? A heart attack? Or something lethal? If so, do you have some unhappy situation smoldering in the background that you are trying to ignore?

☞ Frustrate you? What else is frustrating you?

☞ Embarrass you? Does it make you feel self-conscious? Do you feel like a failure? Does it make you feel you are not good enough?

## CLUE NO. 7:
### THE PART OF THE BODY INVOLVED

Once you understand the way your body serves as a metaphor for expression of inner difficulties, the actual physical site (an arm, a leg and so forth) becomes a source of information.

Here are the parts of the body we want to explore and the issues often involved:

**Face** — self-esteem
**Eyes** — seeing, crying, working
**Ears** — hearing, communications
**Nose** — sensing, breathing
**Upper back** — carrying burdens, grief, sadness
**Chest** — suppressed grief, sadness, heartache
**Lower back** — resentment over mistreatment at work
**Legs and feet** — facing the future, moving ahead in life
**Throat** — communication issues
**Neck** — irritation, conflicts
**Shoulders** — unhappiness at work or in athletics, grief, overload

**Arms, Wrist, Hands** — unhappiness in work
**Skin** — irritation, self-esteem
**Bladder** — suppressed irritation with intimate relationships
**Vagina** — intimacy issues
**Breasts** — nurturing issues, attracting males
**Abdomen** — suppressed fear, anxiety
**Pelvis** — reproductive issues
**Penis** — intimacy issues

Here are some questions to ask yourself:

## THE FACE (SELF-ESTEEM)

☞ Do you have a blemish on your face? Are you in some situation where your appearance is important to you? Could your face be trying to tell you that you're not feeling as confident as you would like to feel?

☞ Is your condition embarrassing? Do you feel insecure? Scared? Inferior to others?

## THE EYES (SEEING, CRYING, WORKING)

☞ Are you trying to avoid seeing something? Are you pushing some awful or unpleasant image or memory out of your mind?

☞ Are your eyes trying to cry? Are you sad? Are you afraid, if you start to cry, you'll cry forever?

☞ Are you uncomfortable with someone at work? Are your eyes helping you escape the situation?

☞ Do you work all day on a computer screen? Does light hurt your eyes? Do your eyes want to close? Have you had all the input you can handle? Do you need quiet time alone?

## EARS (HEARING, COMMUNICATIONS)

☞ Do your ears hurt? Do you need to block out something painful that you don't want to hear? Are you unable to protect yourself from something?

☞ Do your ear canals swell shut? Are they painful?

≳ Do your ears feel plugged but don't hurt? Have you had all the input you can handle? Do you need quiet time? Do you feel obligated to listen to someone?

## Nose (breathing, sensing)

≳ Is your nose running or congested? Is your nose trying to cry?
≳ If you are bothered by allergies, could you be hypersensitive because your feelings are building to the bursting point?
≳ Are you suppressing sadness? Could you be congested with unexpressed feelings?
≳ Have you been minimizing or suppressing things that bother you?
≳ Have you felt unhappy lately?

## Throat (communication issues)

≳ Are you losing your voice? What do you have trouble saying?
≳ Do you have to clear your throat a lot? Do you find it necessary to say things you don't believe?
≳ Do you have to use your voice a lot at work? Have you been angry or upset but can't confront the people involved?
≳ Do you need a break from work? Is your company short-staffed or chronically understaffed?
≳ Are you unsure of or in conflict about what you are saying? Are you afraid someone will get mad or disagree with you?
≳ Are you a teacher?  Are you talked-out? Have you had it with the kids?

## The Neck (irritation, conflicts)

≳ Is someone near you a pain in the neck? Is the pain more apparent when you are with a certain person?
≳ Are you waiting for a settlement for your neck injury? Do you believe the accident ruined your neck? Are you carrying resentment about that? Who do you need to forgive? Have you put your life on hold? Could your injury be helping you avoid facing some situation? Is it earning money for you?

Are you caught in an uncomfortable situation and don't know how to get out of it?

Are you outraged over some situation? What?

## THE SKIN (SELF-ESTEEM ISSUES, IRRITATION)

Does your skin problem make you self-conscious? Do you need to work on self-esteem issues?

Is a rash driving you crazy? Is someone driving you crazy?

How can you resolve this situation?

Are you suppressing anger and irritation? At whom?

## THE UPPER BACK (CARRYING BURDENS, GRIEF, SADNESS)

Are you weighed down by a lot of burdens in life?

Are you laboring to pay off bills? Do you feel like you will never catch up? Are you in conflict over how to do this?

## THE LOW BACK (RESENTMENT OVER TREATMENT AT WORK)

What happened shortly before you injured your back? Do you resent someone at work?

Were you treated unfairly? Disciplined? Yelled at for no reason?

Was your suggestion ignored? Does that burn you up? Did your back problem make them listen?

Does your supervisor have it in for you? Do you hate the sight of him or her?

Are you looking for or are you ready to look for another job? Why?

## THE CHEST (SUPPRESSED GRIEF, SADNESS, HEARTACHES)

Do your chest pains make you feel like crying? What are you

sad about inside?
- Has someone been mean to you lately, or hurt your feelings?
- Are you unhappy about something at work? What happened?
- Have people made a fool of you? Laughed at you?
- Have you lost a loved one? Do you have a relative who is seriously ill?
- Have you had your heart broken lately? Did you convince yourself that you were over your heartache before you really were?

## THE SHOULDERS (UNHAPPINESS AT WORK OR IN ATHLETICS, ALSO GRIEF AND OVERLOAD)

- Does your shoulder pain interfere with any activity? Work? Sports? Do you need to avoid doing something?
- Are you having trouble with your bosses?
- Have you ended a relationship lately? Are you suppressing pain over your relationship? Are you trying not to think about your problem? Have you made yourself too busy?

## THE ARMS, WRISTS, AND HANDS (UNHAPPINESS IN OUR WORK)

- Are you unhappy with something you are doing with your hands: Driving? Art ? Music? Writing? Crafts? Carpentry?
- Are you unhappy in your work?
- Are you looking for another job? Why?
- Do you feel that what you are doing is beneath you? Do you feel like you are doing the right kind of work?

## THE LEGS AND FEET (FACING THE FUTURE, MOVING AHEAD IN LIFE)

- What is coming up? A trip? A move? A competition? Could there be a part of you that dreads it? Do you have mixed feelings?
- Do you feel stuck in an unhappy situation? Do you have trouble facing a problem? Saying what you need to say?
- Do you need to resolve a problem with a relative?

$\backsim$ Have you been dreading cleaning out your deceased spouse's closets or going through his or her things?

## THE ABDOMEN (SUPPRESSED FEAR AND ANXIETY)

$\backsim$ Are you anxious about something that is coming up? A test? A speech? An airplane flight? A party? A family visit? An inspection? A layoff? A competition? Jury duty? A court appearance? A job interview?

$\backsim$ Are you involved in a new relationship? A new job?

## THE BREASTS (NURTURING ISSUES, ATTRACTING MALES)

$\backsim$ Are you nurturing others too much? Not enough? Do you always take care of others without receiving anything in return? Are you draining yourself?

$\backsim$ Do you want sex, intimacy and love, yet hate men? Are you angry at or frightened of men?

$\backsim$ Do you have trouble establishing or sustaining intimate relationships with men? Do you find something wrong with every one of them? Are you afraid of intimacy?

## THE PELVIS (REPRODUCTIVE ISSUES)

$\backsim$ Do you have mixed feelings about getting pregnant or about the number of children you should have? Are you in conflict with your mate about having children?

$\backsim$ Are you stewing over when to have a baby? Are you concerned about your biological clock? Single-parent issues? An absent partner?

## THE BLADDER(SUPPRESSED IRRITATION WITH INTIMATE RELATIONSHIPS)

$\backsim$ Are you angry or irritated at your partner? Why? Is this relationship going too fast? Do you need to back off?

≈ Are you uncomfortable with your intimate life? Would part of you prefer not to have sex? Why? Is pain the only thing that will stop you from having sex?

## THE VAGINA (INTIMACY ISSUES)

≈ Are you scared of being hurt in a relationship or angry because your partner cheated on you? Are you jealous of your partner? Are you too hurt or angry to have sex?

≈ Do you find your partner inept, unsatisfying? Do you need a break from sex and can't say *no*? Is your vagina saying no for you?

## THE PENIS (INTIMACY ISSUES)

≈ Did you cheat on your wife or girlfriend? Do you feel guilty? Can you forgive yourself?

≈ Did you sleep with a prostitute and feel what you did was wrong? Do you feel contaminated?

≈ Do you find your partner unattractive or unstimulating sexually? Is having sex with him/her a chore?

≈ Is your partner too hard to satisfy?

≈ Were you hurt in love? Are you afraid of being hurt again?

≈ Do you need to avoid an intimate relationship?

# CLUE NO. 8:
## THE NATURE OF THOUGHTS, FEARS & BELIEFS

We can create symptoms through the power of our beliefs. Just as our arm can become paralyzed or anesthetized in a hypnotic trance, we can become hypnotized by our own beliefs and in turn bring on all manner of symptoms. We often become convinced we are suffering from something in the environment at work. For instance, chemical exposures, harmful electromagnetic energy fields, repetitive motion, or defective ventilation.

One person develops painful wrists working on a keyboard, and soon half the people in the office have pain in their wrists. One person has headaches, insisting it's due to fumes in the building; soon everyone has headaches. The ailments can be the product of our own thoughts and fears, rather than from physical hazards. Complaints often sweep through offices where the morale is low. I am not suggesting that you ignore known health risks. I am simply suggesting that you be careful what you believe, lest you bring problems on yourself.

In order to explore this area, ask yourself the following questions:

- Did your symptom start shortly after someone else experienced a similar condition? Did you read about the symptom or hear about it on the news?
- Did someone mention something at work that seemed dangerous to you? Did that scare or worry you?
- Do you believe you can catch everything that is going around? That you will get sick if you go outside with a wet head? Catch a chill? Lose sleep? Forget your vitamins?
- Do you believe you have to be careful of what you eat? That your body is sensitive to foods?
- Do you hate the idea of taking medications? Is this why you have problems tolerating them?
- Do you hate the idea of using birth control? Is this why you have problems with every birth-control method you try?
- Do you believe you will hurt your back lifting something? Do you believe your back is delicate? Do you believe it will go out of adjustment easily?
- Are your back pains related to resentment about a work issue?
- Are you afraid that harmful chemicals in your tap water or food are harming you? Do you believe you are suffering from hypoglycemia, candida, Epstein-Barr virus, or chronic fatigue syndrome?
- Could your problems be related to your inner emotional life?
- Could a hidden issue cause your health problems?

The problem is separating truth from falsehoods, scientific fact from superstition. In some parts of the world, people believe in hexes and voodoo dolls. In America, we are frequently preoccupied with toxic exposures and safety concerns that often do not have any basis in fact. It becomes confusing when scientists and specialists disagree.

In going through the questions above, I urge you to write down your *yes* answers. For example, if you answered *yes* to the question about having a delicate back, write down why you believe that.

For example: *My back is damaged as a result of repeated injuries. Now it is weak and unpredictable. Sometimes I can do things without any problem, and other times it goes out if I turn the wrong way or lift the least little thing.*

Such experiences could cause you to believe you have a weak and unstable back. Now that you have begun to understand the role of hidden issues, you need to rethink the probable causes of your back pain.

After thinking it over, you might come up with some thoughts like this: *I recognize that my back pains are real, but I wonder if they are really caused by lifting. I also wonder if my back is really weak and goes out of adjustment easily. Now that I think of it, I have been having problems with my boss at work. Maybe those back pains are related to my resentment and helped me avoid going to work, where I had to face my supervisor. Now that I am working on these issues, my body will no longer need to hurt.*

I encourage you to do the homework and take a careful look at your beliefs about your health. Just reading this book with an open mind will alter your beliefs in a positive direction and bring healing. If your problem persists, consider working with a therapist.

# 19 Using Hypnosis to Uncover Hidden Issues

I t's no wonder most Americans are more than a little frightened at the idea of being hypnotized. The exploitation of hypnotic phenomena by stage hypnotists to amaze and entertain American audiences, combined with Hollywood's melodramatic and often frightening portrayal of hypnosis, have dealt a near-lethal blow to the medical uses of hypnosis in the United States. After all, who wants to be transformed into a zombie-like sleepwalker who mindlessly obeys every command of the hypnotist?

This wariness is reflected in the fact that very few American doctors use hypnosis, and only a small minority of psychotherapists are trained in its use. It is unfortunate, because hypnosis is one of the most powerful forms of natural healing available. In many parts of the world, Australia for example, medical hypnosis is widely taught and a ban on stage hypnotists has helped ensure public acceptance.

Hypnosis is basically a doorway into your unconscious. When you are in your normal waking state, the doorway is usually closed. Your thoughts move in fairly predictable patterns. You think about your shopping lists, jobs, and other tasks. When you go into a hypnotic trance you break out of this habitual way of thinking. While in a hypnotic trance, you have access to memories and feelings that are unavailable during your normal waking state. Your doctor or therapist can use hypnosis to bring them to a conscious level, which is especially useful when dealing with the *iceberg* phenomenon discussed in an earlier chapter. Your old submerged traumas can be contacted, brought to the surface and melted away.

It is similar to going to sleep. Your conscious mind is stilled, and deeper unconscious activity comes forward. Powerful emotions are often expressed in the dream state.

When you go into hypnosis, you do not go to sleep. You are awake and are acutely tuned in to your therapist or doctor at all times. You may vary from basically feeling no different from normal, to a blissful state of relaxation and peace. The deep trance states seem to be intrinsically healing. Just spending time in them is deeply therapeutic. Most of the time, however, you will work at much lighter levels of trance and find it is adequate.

Hypnosis in a therapeutic setting is used mainly to help you connect with your inner feelings, and to help you express and work through what we find there in the way of hidden issues.

While there are several different hypnotic techniques used to uncover suppressed emotional material, there is one in particular that works well when you are dealing with physical symptoms. It is called *ideomotor signaling*, and involves the therapist helping you enter a light trance and then actually asking your unconscious mind to answer *yes* or *no* questions by lifting fingers that have been designated *yes* or *no*. You are very much aware and awake. You can open your eyes and stop the process any time you like. You are not under the control of your therapist; rather, you are working in close cooperation with the therapist.

It can be a bit spooky when something outside your conscious awareness takes over. This implies that your unconscious actually has its own awareness and given the opportunity, can express itself. Of course, your unconscious expresses itself all the time through your body language and through the physical symptoms it gives you.

Your conscious thoughts and desires sometimes influence the finger signals. They are not always accurate. It helps, though, to pose the questions to your inner self, and more often than not, the answers are very revealing.

I usually conduct my interview much along the lines used in this book. Then I instruct the client in the use of the finger signals and help him or her into a trance. After that I simply pose the questions to the client's inner mind:

⟹➤-◊-◄⟸

*Is this back problem related to your relationship with your boss?*
*Is it related to your upcoming wedding?*
*Does your back pain help you get the rest that you need?*

Sometimes my intuition is correct as to where the problem is coming from, and sometimes it's not. The client's inner mind is a great ally in bringing the hidden issue to light. If you want to learn more about this and other hypnotic techniques, read Dr. Gerald Edelstein's *book, Trauma, Trance, and Transformation.*

There are other ways of seeking guidance from the unconscious mind. Many practitioners use muscle testing (kinesiology) to receive *yes-no answers* from the unconscious. A question is posed when the patient is fully conscious, and arm strength is tested. Other practitioners have developed their intuition to the point where they can touch the patient's body and receive information about old traumas stored there.

A complete discussion of hypnotic and other therapeutic techniques is beyond the scope of this book. The important thing to remember is that when talk therapy isn't working, there are other ways to find the cause of your trouble.

# 20 CHINESE MEDICINE & THE MIND-BODY CONNECTION

Like myself, more and more physicians are looking for new ways we can help our patients. Many problems simply don't respond to pills, and hidden issues are hard to address in a busy medical practice. Chinese medicine affords an alternative that approaches the body's deeper process, often helping problems that don't respond to standard western methods. What is Chinese Medicine and how does it work?

First of all, Chinese medicine is more than one thing. Preventive measures include sitting, standing, and walking meditations, breathing practices, and movement exercises like Tai Chi and Qigong. These "qi cultivation" practices come in many forms and variations, and they are used in treatment as well as prevention. Other forms of treatment include acupuncture, acupressure, herbs, and Qigong healing.

Chinese medicine has at its core something from Taoist philosophy called yin/yang theory. The basic idea of yin/yang theory is that everything in our universe is oscillating between opposite qualities. First it is hot, then it is cold; the day breaks and it is light, night falls and it is dark; we are happy, then sad; the ocean is peaceful and calm, then torn by violent storm. Anything pushed to its extreme turns into its opposite. Everything is in a state of flux and seeking balance.

As applied to human health, the theory proposes that the body is seeking a harmonious balance where it will function perfectly. When this balance is disrupted, illness or pain results. Chinese medicine seeks to read the body through various diagnostic methods, then work to restore balance. Then the body fixes itself. The Chinese doctor may use acupuncture, acupressure, massage, herbs, heat applied to acupuncture points by an herbal cigar made of mugwort (moxibustion), skin scraping with a porcelain soupspoon (gua sha), bleeding, or cupping. The amazing thing is that these sometimes primitive-appearing methods often work dramatically. Let me give you an example:

A few years ago I had the opportunity to study a form of Chinese medicine called qigong (pronounced cheegung) healing with Master Fu Wei Zhong, a Chinese qigong master. (There are two types of qigong: qigong exercises, which are done for one's own healing; and medical qigong, which one person performs on another.) For four days we practiced qi cultivation exercises and learned the basics of medical qigong diagnosis and treatment. When I left the initial four-day training, Master Fu looked at me and said in his heavily accented broken English, *You use. Tomorrow, you use.*

The following morning, when I returned to work in my office, a 15-year-old boy returned for his second appointment. He had a bad case of mono: huge swollen tonsils coated with pus, big matted lymph nodes on the back of his neck on both sides, and an enlarged spleen. He had been ill and exhausted for about two weeks. I told him and his mother that his mono test was positive and that there was no treatment other than bed rest for a few weeks. She beseeched me, *Isn't there anything you can do for him?* I told her that if they agreed we could try some qigong healing on him and see if it would help. I explained that in China a severe illness like his would be treated daily, or even twice a day. We bowed to insurance realities and settled on three times in one week. I spent roughly thirty minutes with him and gave him a rather strange looking total body acupressure massage. This is the treatment that Master Fu taught us. It starts on the head, proceeds to the neck and shoulder blades, down the arms, then to the back, down the back of the legs, and up the front of the legs to the abdomen and finally up to the face. The treatment is designed to open and balance the flow of *qi* or spiritual energy in the body.

When I finished he had some color back in his face and his mother said, *Well, that's the first smile I've seen in over a week.* He returned two days later and was much improved. I administered the same treatment. On his final visit three days later, he was completely well. The lymph nodes in the back of his neck had shrunk by half, and what had felt like one huge lump was easily discernible as three separate nodes. I told him to cautiously resume his normal activities, as mono is notorious for relapsing, and treated him again just for good measure. I spoke to his mother a few months later and she told me he remained completely recovered.

This story has been repeated countless times in my practice over the last few years with other cases of mono and many other illnesses. It doesn't work with everything, but it often benefits or cures. A simple qigong treatment on the head and neck relieves headaches roughly 90% of the time. It usually relieves nasal congestion, lasting anywhere from an hour to a week or more. Hay fever symptoms will sometimes clear for as long as a week. I have seen ganglion cysts of the wrist disappear over a period of weeks after a single qigong treatment. Back pain and stiffness are relieved to some degree in almost everyone, sometimes completely.

These methods are simple, effective, and can be learned by anyone. Some people have a natural gift for this kind of work, and it may work better in their hands, but with a few days of instruction on simple techniques and pitfalls, we can all learn to help each other.

Many chronic illnesses are deeply rooted in the body and will not heal with simple qigong methods. Acupuncture takes years of study and clinical experience to master, and an acupuncturist skilled in reading the body's imbalances may be successful where qigong has failed. However, the opposite is true as well. I have treated people successfully with qigong massage, who have failed to benefit from acupuncture.

How does Chinese medicine work to restore balance, and what throws the body out of balance in the first place? Here is where Chinese medicine has an advantage over our western medical model. Chinese medicine posits that our physical body is only the visible outer manifestation of an inner energy the Chinese call *qi*, pronounced *chee*. How do we understand what *qi* is? When I explain Chinese medicine to my patients I start by asking them if they believe they have a soul. In my practice roughly 95% of people say *yes* they do. Then I explain that while the soul is occupying the body, it circulates through a system of channels, namely the acupuncture meridians. The ancients identified these channels through deep meditation practices. There are twelve regular channels. Six come out of the fingers and six come out of the toes, and each is connected to and influences an organ in our body. The most important are the so-called yin organs: the kidney, the heart, the lung, the liver, the spleen, and the master of the heart, or pericardium. These yin organs are each associated with an emotion. Joy with the heart and master of the heart, grief with the lungs, anger with the liver, worry with the spleen, and fear with the kidneys. When imbalances occur with these emotions, the channels and organs connected to them can begin to manifest problems.

What do we mean by *imbalances*? The way the Chinese talk about this is as follows: As we go through life, we encounter one challenge to our spirit after another. These stresses may be child abuse, trouble with a boss, a humiliation, a frightening experience, or any other highly charged event. Some of these experiences are felt and processed completely and are healed, leaving no residue. But none of us are so strong and healthy that we can fully process all the troubles we encounter in life, and the leftover emotional energy gradually accumulates in the channel connected to that emotion. The Chinese call these "accumulations".

These accumulations gradually clog the circulation of spiritual energy through our body. As the balance and free circulation of *qi* is disrupted, the tissues of the body that depend on the normal flow of *qi* begin to suffer. The Chinese talk about tissues being *nourished* by *qi*, and in Chinese medicine pain is thought of as blockage of *qi*. So for example, if there is an imbalance or blockage of qi in the liver channel, a person may get pain along one of the four channels connected to the liver energy: the liver, gallbladder, triple heater, and master of the heart. Headaches tend to be related to an accumulation of anger (liver channel), and it's not a coincidence that the triple heater and gallbladder channels cover the area around and above the eyes, the side of the scalp, and the back of the head and neck.

Does this sound familiar? *Accumulations* are nothing more than the hidden issues we have been talking about. An acupuncturist friend commented to me not long ago when I was describing my methods of working with mind-body issues, that what I was doing was a form of Chinese medicine. Although his training was exclusively in acupuncture and herbs, he immediately related to what I was saying. To his way of thinking, working this way was affecting a change in the *jing*, which can be thought of as the deep waters beneath the more superficial *qi. It's easy to change the qi,"* he said. *"It's much harder to get the change to hold. That takes getting a change in the disturbance in the jing.* This is why in China, severe conditions are treated daily or even twice a day, less serious illnesses every two or three days, and so on. The body is being coaxed back to a healthier way of functioning, but the old pattern keeps trying to reassert itself.

This is where *qi* cultivation practices come into the picture. The more time we invest in breaking up the old unhealthy patterns and cultivating healthy flows of *qi*, the more we move in the direction of health.

What is so fascinating about Chinese medicine is that these *jing* disturbances can sometimes be corrected without any talking whatsoever! I have often marveled at the success achieved in cases that I know or suspect were caused by unhappy situations. The advantage is that these indirect methods completely bypass the defensiveness that so often surfaces, when we attempt to uncover and talk about hidden issues and allow healing to occur. The disadvantage is that if the patient receives no insight into the true cause of his or her problem, the learning and growth may not occur that would allow the person to avoid this type of illness in the future. Mind-body work empowers patients to have the experience of healing themselves simply by taking inventory of their hidden issues, when their old symptom starts to return.

While Chinese medicine may have the advantage of approaching the body's energy in subtle ways to accomplish healing that has eluded western methods, our western culture has the advantage of being more open in talking about our feelings. Western psychology with its many different styles and techniques has long recognized the importance of penetrating the unconscious to uncover and heal old traumas. We are lucky to be witnessing this gentle meeting between East and West. The combination of western medical techniques, Chinese medicine, and modern psychology gives us a potent toolbox for dealing with illness and pain.

# 21 THE MYSTERY OF LOVE

There is one more ingredient in the recipe of healing that I need to talk about, and that is the healing power of love. No book on healing would be complete without talking about love. I believe that ultimately all true healing comes from love. Over and over in my office, I watch people recover from their medical problems just by talking and getting things off their chest. It is the presence of love in the room that allows them to talk. If it wasn't there, they would clam up.

As manifested in the doctor's office, love is being interested in the patient's life. Being interested means asking the right questions..... probing a little deeper. It means taking time. That might even mean sitting down. Early in my career one of my older, established colleagues gave me some advice. *Never sit down,* he said. *It slows you down.*

Sitting down with a patient is a form of love. Getting your eyes out of the chart and into theirs is a form of love. Caring enough to ask that follow-up question that you know is going to keep you in the room with them a lot longer is a form of love. Telling a depressed person that you've been there, too, is a form of love. It helps them to know they're not alone in their suffering.

Love is not always easy. Sometimes it can seem cold. That's tough love, but love it is, if it's guided by wisdom and done out of a desire to help.

Love is goodwill towards a person. Wanting the best for them. Goodwill is the opposite of judgmental, critical thinking. It is telling the overweight person who hates themselves and feels like a failure, that it's not their fault that they can't lose weight and keep it off. Even Oprah can't do it. It's not because they are weak, it's because it's a very difficult thing when your body wants to be heavy. Love is asking the alcoholic if either of his parents have a drinking problem, and letting him know that nine out of ten alcoholics have an alcoholic parent. It's not his fault. Love is having the courage to look a person in the eye who just *enjoys a few drinks* and tell him he has a drinking problem and needs to go to AA.

Love is telling the patient with chronic pain, who has become dependent on narcotics, that you are going to phase him off narcotics. Love is telling him that you know he can do it, and that you are going to decide together just how fast you are going to do it.

Love is being tuned in enough to sense an emotion that's just below the surface and saying, *What's that?* Then it's being quiet and allowing it to come up and out. Love is sitting quietly and letting someone cry, knowing that their tears are necessary for their healing.

Love makes it possible for our pain to come to the surface. It is an energy field. It jars pain loose in people, so they can feel it. The deeper and more unbearable the pain, the more love has to be in the room to contain it. Love makes our pain bearable. Without love our pain is overwhelming. It's too much for us to feel, and it retreats into our subconscious, where it cycles around in our acupuncture meridians making trouble: High blood pressure, diabetes, lupus, multiple sclerosis, arthritis, psoriasis, eczema, allergies, sinusitis, cancer, thyroid disease, and on and on.

Spiritual healing is about love. It is not a trick. Jesus did it with a word and a touch. Anton Mesmer did it with *magnetism,* and countless other healers have done it under different guises and names throughout time. But it is all one thing. Amazing things happen. A patient told me how he came down with diabetes and his neighbor more or less coerced him to go to his church and let their prayer circle pray for him. He thought, *Oh well, it can't hurt,* and his diabetes went away the next day. It never came back. I've heard countless stories about miraculous healing from patients over the years, and I have no doubt that they are true.

It's a great mystery how love heals illness and pain, but isn't it wonderful that it does. Love is transferred to another by a touch, a look, a tone of voice, or a kind word. When two people sit together in silence, love has a chance to enter the room. There is a good feeling that starts to arise. It might be during an acupuncture or acupressure treatment. It might happen when a doctor and patient are doing hypnosis together. Sometimes when I'm hypnotizing a patient, I feel myself being pulled down with them into a wonderful state of relaxation and peace. Simply spending time in this state is a deeply healing experience. It is healing because we have entered the energy field of love, when we feel like this. Illness and pain can't exist in this state. If we can learn to access this place in ourselves we can heal ourselves and others.

The wonderful way we feel in this state is actually an energy field that is contagious. Years ago, I took a series of Tai Chi classes. I was working at the time in an emergency room in a small town hospital. Since I had time to kill between patients, I began practicing Tai Chi in my quarters. With spiritual practices like this, the more you do the better you feel. So soon I was practicing two to three hours a day. I began to feel very relaxed, more relaxed in fact than I had ever felt before. I noticed that when the phone rang to call me to see a patient, I was able to sustain this wonderful feeling on my way to the emergency department by keeping my hand going in a subtle Tai Chi movement. With some practice I was able to maintain this feeling while I interviewed and examined my patients. To my surprise, patients' symptoms started disappearing during my exam. One woman presented with severe stomach pains, and when I laid my hand on her abdomen she said, *What did you do? The pain went away.* I said I didn't do anything, and that I would order some tests to make sure it was nothing serious.

Word got around, and soon the nurses and ambulance crew were asking me to take away their headaches. I would put my hands on their temples, take a breath, and summon that feeling. Sometimes I would say to myself, *think of nothing,* to help the process.

Some people have learned to do this naturally in their life. But most of us are so jangled by the stresses, strains, and *accumulations* of life that we need a little help. This is where a spiritual practice like Tai Chi, Yoga, meditation, self-hypnosis, or Qigong comes in. All of these are aids in helping you enter the energy field of love. The more love you feel, the more love you will spread around. The more we all spread around, the sooner our planet will be healed.

Becoming a more loving person is the greatest task we face in this life. It requires a deep and penetrating honesty with ourselves and others. We must have the courage to admit to ourselves feelings that we wish we didn't have, and to say things to others we wish we didn't have to say. It requires great skill in the art of communication. And it requires great strength, for to become more loving we have to bear the pain of facing our faults and shortcomings, and do the hard work of improving ourselves. To be loving means we have to develop miles of character, for we have to rise above our anger and hurt, and truly forgive those who mistreat us. It requires a lot of attention to our behavior. Whole religions are about this. It requires an ocean of patience and a desire to be kind, both to others and to ourselves.

If we choose the path of love, we are in for it. For love will require much of us and will expose us to emotions of fearsome intensity. Yet it is through the cleansing fire of love that we must go, if we are to be healed.

# Epilogue

# Putting It All Together

# EPILOGUE

e live in an exciting time. We are witnessing the evolution of our understanding of the nature of health and disease. While our advanced medical technology has achieved many wonderful things, people continue to suffer from a myriad of diseases, most of them with unknown causes. Our mechanical model of health has not given us the cures it has promised for so many years, and people sense at a deep level that more and more pills and scans are not the answer to our problems. Alternative approaches to health care are more popular every day as people search for answers. All over the world, health practitioners are attempting to integrate Eastern and Western medical models.

What then are the keys to a healthy life?

At the core of any system of healing has to be an appreciation that you and I are not just these physical bodies. We are a spiritual energy that occupies these bodies. A soul if you will. We are here on earth encountering life in all its beauty and intensity. We experience love, hate, despair, grief, pain, frustration, joy, agony, sorrow, and every other feeling state imaginable. The idea that all that intensity goes on without affecting the physical container defies common sense. This is the first key: your body is affected by your emotional experience of life.

I've talked about the unconscious mind. An acceptance of the reality of the unconscious is the second key to health. You have an unconscious mind. You don't know what's in there. That's why it's called unconscious. An openness to the idea that your own unconscious material might be causing your illness allows you to begin exploring in that direction. It allows you to begin developing the personal skills necessary to process powerful, often unpleasant emotions and work through them. Everyone has been overwhelmed at some time by powerful emotions. Our inborn survival mechanisms have dealt with this by compartmentalizing these feelings in the unconscious. Out of sight, out of mind. I've tried to help bring these past experiences to your awareness in the portion of this book dealing with case histories.

Unconscious material won't come to the surface unless we are in a safe and caring environment with a person or persons we trust. It can't be rushed. When others open up and share their deepest feelings, it gets us in touch with ours. This is the third key. We need each other. You need to establish a trusting relationship with a person or group with whom you can share your deepest, most vulnerable feelings.

The fourth and final key I will talk to you about is the fact that help is available for you from your inner mind. That same unconscious that is so protective of your deepest needs in volunteering such a variety of helpful symptoms is prepared to work with you to get you well. It is a deep well of wisdom regarding your own inner truth. It knows what you need. It knows what your symptoms mean, and what they have been accomplishing for you, if anything. And it will tell you if you ask. Those who can pray, and ask for help from their highest spiritual source, or from spiritual guides or angels, tap into this same well of wisdom and guidance. Use the questions in Part III as a guide and, with the help of a therapist familiar with this kind of work, pose *yes-no* questions to your inner mind. Remember that if you have been coping with symptoms you will need to learn some new behaviors as you release the old patterns. That is why you must work with your therapist so you can practice new ways of dealing with challenging situations. This takes time and patience.

My heart will be with you on your exciting journey to a healthier, happier life. But please, take a friend along; don't try to make the trip alone.

# INDEX

## P

pelvic pain  51
pimples  120
pink eye  18-19
pleurisy  101
positive thinking  10

## R

repetitive motion injuries  29
resentment  41, 43-46

## S

school performance  37
self-esteem  109-110
shortness of breath  75
shoulder pain  83, 86, 87, 95
skin rash  11, 18, 73, 74, 84, 114
sore throat  25, 46
sprained ankle  47
stomach pains  47, 167
stress  3, 68
swallowing  23
swelling  74

## U

uveitis  26

## V

vaginal problems  23, 35-36,
    111-113, 115, 116-117, 120-121
vertigo  67, 75
vomiting  65

## W

warts  27, 123-125
weakness  67-69
will power  29
writer's block  109-110
wry neck  92-93
wry neck  107

## Y

yeast infections  120-122